Poetry Ireland Review 117
Eagarthóir / Editor
Vona Groarke

© Poetry Ireland Ltd 2015

Poetry Ireland Ltd/Éigse Éireann Teo gratefully acknowledges the assistance of The Arts Council/An Chomhairle Ealaíon and The Arts Council of Northern Ireland.

Poetry Ireland invites individuals and commercial organizations to become Friends of Poetry Ireland. For more details, please contact:

Poetry Ireland Friends Scheme, Poetry Ireland, 32 Kildare St, Dublin 2, Ireland

or telephone +353 1 6789815; e-mail management@poetryireland.ie

FRIENDS:
Joan and Joe McBreen, Desmond Windle, Neville Keery,
Noel and Anne Monahan, Ruth Webster, Maurice Earls,
Mary Shine Thompson, Seán Coyle, Henry and Deirdre Comerford

Poetry Ireland Review is published three times a year by Poetry Ireland Ltd. The Editor enjoys complete autonomy in the choice of material published. The contents of this publication should not be taken to reflect either the views or the policy of the publishers.

ISBN: 1-902121-58-9
ISSN: 0332-2998

ASSISTANT EDITOR: **Paul Lenehan** with the assistance of **Maggie McDowell**, **Catherine Ward** and **Orla Higgins**

IRISH-LANGUAGE CONSULTANT: **Liam Carson**

DESIGN: **Alistair Keady (www.hexhibit.com)**

COVER CREDIT: *Boolakeel: the mountain wandered off sometimes*, etching, 9.5 x 9.5 cm, by **Niamh Flanagan (www.niamhflanagan.com)**

Contents — Poetry Ireland Review 117

Vona Groarke	5	EDITORIAL
Damian Smyth	7	THE KILCLIEF PISSARROS
	8	THE BACK ROAD TO STRUELL
Stav Poleg	9	JORDAN VALLEY
Armel Dagorn	10	AFTER ALL THESE NIGHT BUSES
	11	ON THE MADHOUSE GROUNDS WITH ALEXIS
D Nurkse	12	THIS LIFE
Beverley Bie Brahic	13	REVIEW: MAUREEN N MCLANE, KEVIN YOUNG, CLAUDIA RANKINE, VIJAY SESHADRI
GC Waldrep	18	WOUNDSINGER
	19	TO THE LOVERS OF DAMAGE
Ellen Cranitch	20	THE RAZOR
Kevin Higgins	21	QUESTION ASKED ME BY YOUNG WOMAN WHO RECENTLY WON A MARATHON
Tara Bergin	22	REVIEW: GABRIEL ROSENSTOCK, FRED JOHNSTON, THEO DORGAN
Frances Galleymore	25	STORY
Ian Pople	26	THE END OF APRIL
John Wedgwood Clarke	27	RENOVATION
David Butler	28	AND THEN THE SUN BROKE THROUGH
Interview	29	COLETTE BRYCE INTERVIEWS GWYNETH LEWIS
Libby Hart	38	HIS COUNTRY IS CALLING ME
Enda Coyle-Greene	39	THAT BLUE TIME
Killian O'Donnell	40	GOLDEN BRIDGE
Emer Fallon	41	SCATTERBRAIN
Alice Lyons	42	REVIEW: FRANCES LEVISTON, PETER SIRR
Simon Ó Faoláin	46	ZEITGEIST
Ceaití Ní Bheildiúin	47	MATAMAITIC DO SHIANSA ÁR N-ANAMA
	49	TAR AGUS TÓG
Paddy Bushe	50	REVIEW: CATHAL Ó SEARCAIGH
Mary Melvin Geoghegan	55	THE RAIN AT THE WINDOW
Nerys Williams	56	BIBLIOPHILE
Patrick Deeley	57	POULTICE
Aidan Rooney	58	IN A COUNTRY CHURCHYARD
Caitríona O'Reilly	59	REVIEW: DENNIS O'DRISCOLL
Joanna Guthrie	64	SMALL HOURS
John Murphy	65	BIRD
Tom French	66	NORTH OF THE VILLAGE
	67	OWENDUFF
Henri Cole	68	REVIEW: SEAMUS HEANEY
Kevin Graham	72	TRACES
Martina Evans	73	EVERYTHING INCLUDING THIS ROOM IS A FUTURE RUIN
Luke Morgan	75	CRIB MOBILE

Paul Batchelor	76	REVIEW: LOUISE GLÜCK, PETER FALLON
Maurice Harmon	80	FLIGHT
Liane Strauss	81	THE GATEKEEPERS
Anne Tannam	82	FERAL
Lucy Collins	83	REVIEW: EAVAN BOLAND, GERALD DAWE, PEGGY O'BRIEN
Annabel Luery	87	GOLDCREST
David Sergeant	88	THE DOGLEG CORNISH LANES
Cherry Smyth	89	FIRST FLOOR CONVERSION
Ciaran Berry	90	REVIEW: KEI MILLER, DERYN REES-JONES, HUGO WILLIAMS
David Wheatley	94	from MAKING STRANGE
Jared Harel	102	MASTERS OF THE UNIVERSE
Alan Gillis	103	REVIEW: *AFTER THE TITANIC: A LIFE OF DEREK MAHON*
Kathleen O'Brien	110	WILD IRIS
Macdara Woods	111	IN TOMIS HE REMEMBERS
Tomas Unger	112	HAY
Desmond Graham	113	THE CHANGELING
Kevin MacNeil	114	REVIEW: DERMOT HEALY
John O'Donnell	119	REVIEW: ANTHONY CRONIN, ENDA WYLEY, NESSA O'MAHONY
Michael Longley	122	IN THE MUGELLO
	123	KINDLING
	124	THE CHESTNUT PAN
Eiléan Ní Chuilleanáin	125	REVIEW: *28 PORTUGUESE POETS*, ANTONELLA ANEDDA, RENÉ CHAR
Interview	129	NELL REGAN INTERVIEWS SEAMUS MURPHY
Notes on Contributors	137	

Editorial

You'd expect a squall, a downpour, a flurry of poems about winter in this job. We live northernly, after all, with nights that settle into stanzas of darkness punctuated by short, pallid breaks of what some would call daylight. Five months of it, give or take, if you measure time as we make clocks do, between the hour harking back and the same hour tripping over itself to face forward, five months on. Never mind spring and autumn: in this neck of the woods, they seem so often seasons in disguise, half-heartedly throwing shapes that don't rightly belong to them.

It's not as if there's very much else to do (is there?) but to apply language to that darkness, to make sense or music of it, to make the ends of it meet. An indoor season. A private season. A season for looking out through cold windows, for noticing, as DH Lawrence did, 'December's bare iron hooks sticking out of earth', and to spite them, pulling fast around us whatever comfort is to hand. A season for the rubbing together of words to strike a warmth to get you through. For the noise the world makes when it freezes or blusters or crouches or stalls.

Winter is the outside and inside of sound, the hard blow and the surge of darkness set against the spidery tinkle of frost on the side of the road. Winter is sound the way summer is colour. 'Winter solitude / ', Bashō writes (via Robert Hass): 'in a world of one colour / the sound of wind'. Winter songs are difficult songs, and sometimes it seems that all the words have the clench of ice in them. 'Like brooms of steel / The Snow and Wind / Had swept the Winter Street', as Emily Dickinson has it, and those brooms of steel are what I hear in the wind against my bedroom window, these big weather nights on Winter Street.

Winter Street is dark, of course: Hermes broke all the streetlamps with stones on his way Underground to rescue Persephone. He's like that, is Hermes, patron of thieves. He forgets he's also patron of travellers, who might be glad of an obliging light to ward off the thieves. Perhaps he's conflicted: how can you tend equally to both traveller and thief?

Or maybe he's been trying his arm (again) at catching Euturpe's eye, fashioning a darkness for her that she might strike a light of her own. Muse of elegiac poetry, she knows the truth of Margaret Atwood's claim that 'writing has to do with darkness, and a desire or perhaps a compulsion to enter it, and, with luck, to illuminate it, and to bring something back out to the light'.

You'd think such elegant ambitions and intricate music would call on an equal poetry and that together, dressed in their best scarves and mittens, they'd skitter out to play. But doesn't it seem like spring gets all the best lines, and the heartiest, most zealous poems? Nothing is so beautiful, Fr. Hopkins says. (Whereas the most cheerful news he has of winter is, 'The times are nightfall, look, their light grows less; / The times are winter, watch, a world undone.') In Spring, Philip Larkin (not usually known as a gusher) hears, 'Begin afresh, afresh, afresh'. And what, by comparison, does winter get? All those hours of soulful fire gazing, of being skinned to the bone by ice and wind, of leavening out the rations and stockpiling summer hopes, and what do we have at the end of it? Ogden

Nash: 'I knew one hound that laughed all winter / At a porcupine that sat on a splinter'.

Which would be plenty, god knows, but it is not all. Here's US poet, Linda Gregg, making – in 'Winter Love' – a house of silence in which nothing quite rises to its occasion and yet, something about its small efforts and half failures rings true to the way this most demanding of seasons must be negotiated, however clumsily.

> I would like to decorate this silence,
> but my house grows only cleaner
> and more plain. The glass chimes I hung
> over the register ring a little
> when the heat goes on.
> I waited too long to drink my tea.
> It was not hot. It was only warm.

It's thin enough on the ground, the poetry of winter, warm when it should be hot, maybe, sparse when lavish is called for. Perhaps that's only as it should be, poetry following the rule of nature, like any living thing. But against that, I give you the final two stanzas of Rita Dove's 'November for Beginners', a poem that does what few poems manage, in making music of decline.

> So we wait, breeding
> mood, making music
> of decline. We sit down
> in the smell of the past
> and rise in a light
> that is already leaving.
> We ache in secret,
> memorizing
>
> a gloomy line
> or two of German.
> When spring comes
> we promise to act
> the fool. Pour,
> rain! Sail, wind,
> with your cargo of zithers!

A cargo of zithers: it's as good a description as any of a poetry magazine, (and probably better than some). I hope the music of the poems herein helps somehow to decorate a silence for you, and to make light of winter hours.

Vona Groarke

Damian Smyth

THE KILCLIEF PISSARROS

It happens that all that is known of these people
Is what ends up inscribed at their heads
In marble or stone and frequently wood;
Or what is remembered by the few who knew them,
Descendants, inheritors, even the strangers
Who build on the property and find concealed
In the walls or under the floorboards tokens
Of love, shots fired, small, routine betrayals,
Before that narrative resource too dwindles
And is gone at a stroke: futility of seed.
They have in fact been wind farmers for ever,
For all their elegant shadows across fields
Are gathered in by the embrace of the blades
Above the dead aerodrome, travelling nowhere.
Who are they? Where have they come from? Where going?
Into the town on tractors, mainly: Lidl-poachers,
Off-License harvesters; ironmonger beachcombers;
Aisle reachers and stretchers; pioneers of the road
Each single day; assemblers at the hilltop; buriers.
There is nowhere to go but to the open window
And stare out at them or they to this window staring in
At what are just words, putting names to faces,
Calling them sojourners, matriarchs, ancestors,
Comrades somehow who occasionally dance.
How they resort though to the universe of tarmac
Lit with the ethics of yellow ochre and blue,
Livestock thumping the tassels of fuchsia, red diesel,
Afterglow of bouquets decayed at bad corners,
Having their thought and finishing it outside.

Damian Smyth

THE BACK ROAD TO STRUELL

Now that the road to the wells behind the Mental –
Those fields of asphodel indeed, those gardens
Of fuchsia and mint and delinquent wild rose
Tended by the lost and the unforgiven, by the baffled
And abandoned – has been closed off by police,
There is nowhere I might meet my father by design
Or accident, even if I travelled to the waters
At the appointed hour, before dawn at Easter
Or St John's Eve when, it is said, the waters rise
To flood the stone enclosure magically
Though tidal shifts and seasonal rain account
For the sacred transubstantiation, seemingly.
But it's still out on the road such meetings happen:
The act of travelling itself, a kind of leaving home
That mimics theirs and makes half-possible
Their step out from the hedges, almost missed,
The dead retaining the modesty of their lives
In extremis and beyond, arriving unannounced,
Looking in, their final mortal fracas far behind them.
It makes sense now that they are out there always:
Where else but every place they were at home,
Considered, spoken of, now literally recalled?
It's those who have survived love age and weaken,
More transient, less persistent, more easily dissuaded.
If he waits there, it's without surprise and once again in vain.

Stav Poleg

JORDAN VALLEY

Press your palm into the sunburnt skin of grass,
into the fields of 38 June Celsius.
Watch how the trees turn into silhouettes,
the cropped wheat spines breathe out
leftover salt and turquoise that is out of turquoise,
is almost white.

The valley sinks into the mountains' yellow shades,
into a summer hibernation,
six months without a drop of rain, just memories
of rain, as if all winters come with stories,
and when you shut the valley's door and light a cigarette,
I'll tell you mine.

Armel Dagorn

AFTER ALL THESE NIGHT BUSES

through the Andes we forget
some hotels don't barrel down
mountainsides and then creep up
when the world rises again.
In the drowned glow of the odd
village street lamp or moon ray
through curtains we compare,
to pass the time, the companies,
the best buses where stewards
dish out airplane fare
on plastic trays, and synthetic
blankets to keep us warm
and entertained, their static
electric feel turning our fingertips
into fireflies, and the others,
in which the cold wind reaches us
through cracks, and sheep and chicken
coop in the hold, herded in
with our backpacks, making us
feel like we're the last
Noahs in the world, aiming
for the shelter of summits
Incas once believed were gods.

Armel Dagorn

ON THE MADHOUSE GROUNDS WITH ALEXIS

In our days of hopping walls
all over town, of creeping up alleys
when all the cats are grey stray
blurs fleeing, of hanging outside
the bakery's back door and waiting
for the very first croissant of the day
to be handed down to us
like a blessing,
picking up our bedtime with buttery hands
where upright citizens left theirs behind
to man and woman offices and machinery,
we once ended up on a bench,
on an expansive, walled-in lawn
we'd been seeing for years,
the backdrop of the nursery school
we'd given our custom to,
a landscape never questioned
until we sat inside it,
our young brains already nostalgic
but totally unburdened
by what the future might bring,
by the idea that fate or whatever
rather than our own restless feet
might pick us pawns up
then one square further
lay us down, mate, in a dark spot.

D Nurkse

THIS LIFE

After swimming in Kiln Lake we were so tired,
you and I, we dried ourselves with the nubby red towel
that smells of dog, then slept side by side
in the tall grass, careless of ticks – when we woke
it was this life, we dried each other again
with our fingertips, Venus had risen, and a red star
whose name I don't know, Antares or Betelgeuse:
as always we waited for a sign, let this life
be a sign: we heard the frogs calling, almost ranting,
and saw no one, the rushes bent to our shape,
a glow-worm, two clumps of breathing earth.

Beverley Bie Brahic

ALL YOU LIKE: FOUR AMERICAN POETS

Maureen N McLane, *This Blue* (Farrar, Straus, Giroux, 2014), $14.
Kevin Young, *Book of Hours* (Alfred A Knopf, 2014), $16.95.
Claudia Rankine, *Citizen: An American Lyric* (Graywolf Press, 2014), $20.
Vijay Seshadri, *3 Sections* (Graywolf Press, 2013), hb $22.

American poetry often feels to me like one of those eat-all-you-want buffets: too many variables. How to choose among the hot and cold plates of autobiographical, perceptual, conceptual, surreal, formal and deconstructed? Minimal, baroque? Fast food, slow food? Fusion? The mind boggles. Still, a few poets stand out, notably John Ashbery, whose magpie nests of shiny linguistic objects feel avant-garde even today. And the mid-Atlantic Paul Muldoon whose virtuoso poem shapes and *New Yorker* editorship have amplified contemporary American poets' interest in rhyme and the kind of language play that puts paid to Puritan earnestness. But when critics look for what will make it new in twenty-first century American poetry, they – flummoxed, taking sides? – variously forecast a return to the hierarchies of syntax, to the outward-looking, irony-eschewing lyrics of a William Carlos Williams (Creeley, Niedecker), and to narrative – all poetics that can feel more like retrenchment. What is not clear is where the weight of experimentation after Ashbery tends. 'The new poetry will look nothing like the old', the conceptual poet and author of *Uncreative Writing* Kenneth Goldsmith proclaimed in an April 2015 *Poetry* (Chicago) manifesto: 'The internet is the greatest poem ever written.'

    Maureen McLane's third collection, *This Blue,* taps into diverse veins of literary history, but her voice – tender, intelligent, self-deprecating, amused – is all her own. *This Blue* arrives on the heels of *My Poets,* her book *about* poetry, and has enviable airiness: much of it happens in the white space between the lines; sometimes words trail off into tantalizing ellipses, encouraging the reader to mind the gaps; jump cuts let her veer between apparently disparate motifs without resorting to the cumbersome syntax of propositional logic and narrative. Time and place may be indeterminate, human beings wear only pronouns. All this makes for suggestiveness and fluidity. Occasionally one longs for more weight.

    Other features of *This Blue*: playfulness with sounds, rhyme: 'Why the low mood, / the picking at food?' ('What's the Matter'); eroticism ('a boy's succulent anus /... call it ranunculus ... the folded rose / whose folds your nose / now probes' ('All Good'). Poems are mostly short-lined, with or without stanzas, although McLane, when she uses longer lines, sounds authoritative too. At titles she's a wizard. Earthy, she enjoys the outdoors with bees and meadows and comfy chairs ('Morning with Adirondack Chair'), as much as to say pastoral, but she can write about ideas and – sparingly – cities.

What fascinates me is the way McLane, with an appealing absence of self-importance, incorporates a range of discourse. Here she is in 'Late Hour' observing insect life in the grass, and making big statements (note the witty line breaks, the clash of dictions) in an offhand manner:

> isn't it time
> to say the garden
> is wasted
>
> on us? untended
> roses the Japanese
> beetles gone
>
> apeshit the labor
> theory of value
> will not redeem
>
> the labor required
> to reclaim
> this.

'I think there's something very interesting in the rehabilitation of the simple', McLane has said. 'Simple' may be disingenuous. McLane's simplicity is that of the gifted couturier.

The bad news about Kevin Young's *Book of Hours* is that there are far too many poems (for a poetry book it's a Russian novel), and many are slight and repetitive. Still it is thoughtfully, if unsurprisingly, arranged with an arc that runs, unsurprisingly, from the death of the poet's father, in the first section, to the birth of his son, in the third, and closes with a more abstract group of lyrics on time and landscape. The narrative sections show Young to be a poet capable of writing about loss with the sort of comic detail that makes grief more poignant: 'So many socks ... and still, / father, you have errands, / / errant dry cleaning to pick up' ('Charity'). But this is familiar territory, even if Young's male, minority stance brings a fresh tonality to his material. The most original work here may be his pregnancy poems. During a prenatal visit ('Expecting') he and his wife listen to their son's heartbeat:

> You are like hearing
> hip-hop for the first time – power

> hijacked from a lamppost – all promise.
> You couldn't sound better, break-
> dancer, my favorite song bumping
>
> from a passing car.

'Labor Day' also harnesses a fresh set of metaphors and the quick-fire cadences of television commentary to a subject more often claimed as female territory: 'It's knotted in the ninth / after a double sends Manny / home for the Sox // … you're into / extra innings too – / days overdue – / stranded on base // like machinery / on the moon'. The water-colour translucency of the final lyrics …

> The light here leaves you
> lonely, fading
>
> […]
>
> This valley belongs
> to no-one –
>
> except birds who name
> themselves by their songs

… speak to the poet's presence in the world differently than the family poems. But whether he is writing figuratively or attending, in a more Heideggerian vein to the natural world, Young is a generous, celebratory poet whose last words are 'Why not sing'.

Claudia Rankine is a Jamaican established in the US whose riveting book *Citizen: an American Lyric* confronts racism head-on. It doesn't fit any standard definition of a poetry collection, filled as it is with texts, mostly untitled, that range from the vignette style and length of the Baudelairean prose poem to a 14-page analytical document about the black tennis player, Serena Williams. Rankine contemplates and probes her and others' reactions to 'ordinary' racism in a deceptively low key, and her anger is all the more powerful – explosive – for seeming contained:

> You are in the dark, in the car, watching the black-tarred
> street being swallowed by speed; he tells you his dean
> is making him hire a person of color when there are so
> many great writers out there.

Interspersed with visual art, some texts are scripts for video about events like the 2012 shooting of Trayvon Martin, the World Cup, or Hurricane

Katrina (2006), the last an assemblage of quotes from CNN:

> Faith, not fear, she said. She'd heard that once and was
> trying to stamp the phrase on her mind. At the time she
> couldn't speak it aloud. He wouldn't tolerate it. He was
> angry. Where were they? Where was anyone? This is a
> goddam emergency, he said.

Made in collaboration with the filmmaker John Lucas, these share an aesthetic with Kenneth Goldsmith's work (see his *Seven American Deaths and Disasters*) in their appropriations of language from the media. Even at her most conventionally lyrical Rankine is edgy, as in this more traditionally inward moment:

> Some years there exists a wanting to escape –
> you, floating above your certain ache –
> still the ache coexists.
> Call that the immanent you ...
>
> [...]
>
> you're not sick, not crazy,
> not angry, not sad –
>
> It's just this, you're injured.

Citizen won the 2015 Forward Prize for Poetry and was a finalist for the US National Book Award. I read it in a single sitting. It took the top of my head off, even though the words that compose the poem-book seem banal. Maybe that's the secret.

Vijay Seshadri was born in Bangalore and grew up American. *Three Sections* (there are no sections) won the Pulitzer Prize, and no need to read beyond the 11-line opening poem, 'Imaginary Number,' to understand why:

> The mountain that remains when the universe is destroyed
> is not big and not small.
> Big and small are
>
> comparative categories, and to what
> could the mountain that remains when the universe is destroyed
> be compared?

> Consciousness observes and is appeased.
> The soul scrambles across the screes.
> The soul,
>
> like the square root of minus 1,
> is an impossibility that has its uses.

'Imaginary Number' sets up the penultimate poem, a 16-page tour de force called 'Personal Essay' that at times recalls Eliot's *Four Quartets,* at others Ashbery's *Self Portrait in a Convex Mirror*, while being completely its own beast: a mixture of rant and meditation that attempts to think about the human condition while travelling in a cab between home and airport, and concludes: 'The world is huge and unbearable to think about'. In between these two poems are poems with titles like 'Purgatory, the Film', 'Bright Copper Kettles' (no copper kettles) and a long expository-descriptive, *New Yorker*-ish prose piece about commercial salmon fishing in the north Pacific.

I should say that this is a very funny book. Seshadri has a wonderfully dry sense of humour; hyperbolic flights of fancy and encyclopedic lists end with hilarious recalls to reality and pratfalls: 'The scent of honeysuckle floated from the garden … / from which garden was heard voices and the sound of birds … / And on Atlantic Avenue, in a cab going to the airport'. Like Elizabeth Bishop, or Philip Larkin in some of his most expansive, least propositional poems ('Here', 'Show Saturday'), Seshadri takes immense pleasure in detail, for its own sake, rather than as symbol or metaphor: 'the sweet ripe peach, dripping honey, / the salmon trollers anchored up in the cove /…the historical figures / … don't *resemble* anything. They're just themselves.' (Or, as Elizabeth Bishop wrote, 'Everything only connected by "and" and "and".') These are the poems of a single self, but that self is under almost unbearable strain to hold it all together, not fly off into a zillion pieces, meanwhile undercutting the deadly seriousness of the enterprise with laughter. *Three Sections* is an example of that rare book that is at once witty and affecting.

GC Waldrep

WOUNDSINGER

It is the littlest details
that make beauty
bearable. A clock's
perfect hands
tied behind
your lover's back.
A storm in the distance
like a bruise
rising to the surface
of someone else's
tragedy. In the super-
market I dreamt
I stood on three legs.
Then a woman
came, and changed me.
Now I walk
in the dark. All I can
do is keep walking.
Notice the vintage
metalwork,
the way the nails
pierce each signature
individually. I woke
into a bronze
wavelength, a black-
smith's grainy muscle.
A bit of light
in Soutine's childhood
hanging like meat.
My lover
lies far away,
on a bed of jasper.
She is perfect
the way pain is perfect.
Speak ark, speak ash.
Invite a thief
into this great house.

GC Waldrep

TO THE LOVERS OF DAMAGE

you burn golden like a fog like a fever in a movie
a silver cradle hung between us, I placed a book in it
I buried every red piece
I grew flat within it, like a drawing

in the cartoon I found in that broken church, love
was played by a man, but
when she touches me
she coaxes a threshing music, a gilt
from whatever I am able to bless or barter

– the cradle, the book, the awl
with which I pierce this flesh I wear, as if from music
breath could draw its final victory
I poured a ship into an arbour, & called that
'peace be to the winter hive'
(losing sight slowly of the Rio Grande, its green hilt)

I would tangle myself with you I would pray
to every king alone tonight in his garden
warming his hands
(although he does not know it)
at your harrow, your breast, your veiling, your eye

Ellen Cranitch

THE RAZOR

Coming in from the South, blown in
on a cone of air and a hangover,

my heart's salmon-leap at the sight of it,
all city glitter, all liquid supple thing.

Head, shear-diagonal; body, lipstick-
columnar, tongued turbines sift air

just like abacus beads create streaming
numbers and my thoughts shift to beauty,

to pure abstraction. Hungerford Bridge:
barred light, straps of shade, slab me in.

Quick, fix it, reach back to it, hold the turbines –
which flip, line up coin-rim-flat, deliver

a triple, perfect-oval sky; and the heart-gasp of it,
shock-through of it, pierces, gifts me joy.

Kevin Higgins

QUESTION ASKED ME BY YOUNG WOMAN WHO RECENTLY WON A MARATHON

And do you run?
        From the sound of this
cough, I'm running nowhere
        except out of time. Since
Mom left to debate the finer points
        with Lady Gregory and William Joyce
– late of Rutledge Terrace
        and the Third Reich – up there
in the Cemetery; I'm aware,
        for the likes of me, more is gone
than is to come.

        I expect, any year now,
to fall off that ladder
        I never go up,
to be staring blankly on the path
        when whoever it is finds me.
Or one morning in the bathtub
        to clutch hard both my rubber duck
and my anus, as I'm struck
        by a terror cold as the North Sea.
Then, slack-jawed, letting go.
        Everything. All at once.

Tara Bergin

ART IS FAITH

Gabriel Rosenstock, *Sasquatch* (Arlen House, 2013), €12.99.
Fred Johnston, *Alligator Days* (Revival Press, 2013), €10.
Theo Dorgan, *Nine Bright Shiners* (Dedalus Press, 2014), €12.99.

Authenticity has become a problematic standard by which to judge poetry. Like sincerity, the term has come to have too many bad associations, implying that it is only by a legitimacy of origin that a work can be deemed worthwhile. Yet the word 'authentic' is broader than this, and less simplistic. It also means 'trustworthy', 'one acting on one's own authority', literally, 'self-do-er', and it is with these definitions in mind that I would like to use the word to describe all three titles under review here. This is because each appears to have at its source not only a deep and true relationship with poetry and poetic language, but also a genuine belief in the value of the individual's pursuit, through that language, of locating what Wordsworth called the 'breath and finer spirit' of knowledge.

The first example of this, then, is Gabriel Rosenstock's *Sasquatch*, a full-length, linked sequence of very short, bilingual, sparsely punctuated, lyrical poems. In their apparent shunning of ornament or artifice, their spirituality, and their mixture of simplicity and esotericism, these poems share many features with the sayings, riddles, and epigrams that are found in traditional verse forms. What is admirable about a collection such as this is that it offers cohesion, accessibility and approachability, while remaining mysterious. Indeed the brevity of the poems – the longest is sixteen lines, the shortest three – means that mystery need not shut out the reader but rather invite the reader in. In other words, it offers a language of secrecy, but it also gives us the key to understanding the secret.

The sasquatch is a Bigfoot character who observes the world as if experiencing it for the first time. Following sasquatch's journey amongst birds, trees, fire, and sky, these poems are marked by a sense of longing, a desire for unmediated connection with the elements. The form and style of writing echoes this: it too is utterly concentrated on remaining elemental, as if it wished to compromise on nothing. Here, for instance, is a three-line poem called 'Fences' / 'Sconsaí', quoted in its entirety: 'When he first saw them / he didn't know / what they were' ('Nuair a leag sé súil i dtosach / orthu níor thuig sé / cad ab ea iad'). Here is another, called 'Crescent Moon' / 'Gealach Dheirceach': 'Who is eating it? / Who is eating it? / Who is eating the moon?' ('Cé atá á hithe? / Cé atá á hithe? / Cé atá ag ithe na gealaí?'). A child might have asked these questions, and this is a clue to the poetry's purpose: Rosenstock is on a quest to return to something primitive, something prior to learning, in order to expose the truth. This book represents a crisis of sorts, both of language and spirit, but it is one which results in clarity, and a kind of peaceful, if final, reincarnation in 'Clouds Gather':

> birth and death
> birth and death again and again
>
> now the sky clears:
> I know I shall be born no more

Fred Johnston's latest collection, *Alligator Days*, shares something with Rosenstock's *Sasquatch*, in the sense that it too represents a serious reflection on the world and how we conduct ourselves within it. Yet in terms of style and form, the difference is marked. Where Rosenstock's poems strive towards poise and stillness, Johnston's are full of noise, and movement, and clamour, and they make their impression this way. Compared to the clean and clear language of *Sasquatch*, Fred Johnston's vision is strikingly un-gentle: 'There is the rock-*meister's* house', the book begins, 'gaudy on the sea-shore, / perched like a parrot on a toilet-bowl' ('Alligator Days'). It seems ugly but there is a discernible rhythm to it, and as the book continues, it is clear that this rhythmic quality is a strong point of the collection as a whole. See for instance the poem 'A Cheese Sandwich is Very Forgiving', whose playful title and ordinary setting is underpinned with music, and philosophy:

> He found a seat at a round white table with a view
> Of the river, and here he sat over a coffee and a cheese
> Sandwich and remembered that he was a man.

Johnston's humour, and self-humour, makes the profundity of the best poems even more effective. There is a formality of structure and a careful attention to sound which is constantly offset and energized by the use of everyday imagery. Subject-matter includes supermarkets, porn, credit unions, writing, love, and a golf-ball – a golf-ball which Johnston manages to describe in a poetic and moving way, 'the white uncrackable egg no bird laid /... trying to hide / in its nest in the earth and always pulled out' ('To Watch a Man Playing Golf'). This alone is evidence of the originality and energy of this collection.

Nine Bright Shiners, the title of Theo Dorgan's latest collection, comes from 'Green Grow the Rushes O!' a traditional counting song in which number nine is 'nine for the nine bright shiners'. The phrase is said by some to refer to the planets, though there are other interpretations. As a song it is a strange yet compelling blend of nursery-rhyme and folklore: on the one hand popular and childish; on the other hand sophisticated and symbolic; it could be a lullaby, or a warning song; a devotional song, or a song about war. Whatever the answer, it serves as a suitable starting point for this collection, which is very often song-like, nearly always rhythmical, and regularly makes use of refrain, rhyme, and narration. These poems represent a communication, on various levels, with the poets of the past, as well as with Irish history, and the Ireland of the present. It does so in such a whole-hearted, whole-spirited way that its *authenticity* is unquestionable.

The collection opens with 'The Angel of History': a figure in a 'long loose coat' who appears before the poet holding a notebook and crossing off the names of 'Senators, Deputies, Ministers'. When the vision disappears into the rain, the poet, having witnessed this 'cold, exact cancellation', walks home, 'afraid for my country'.

Afraid, but not fearful. Dorgan's poems are built on a high note of intensity, and in this way they prove themselves: 'I light my candles to human love', he writes in 'Family Tree' – a genealogical chart which includes Lorca, Dante, and Nadezhda Mandelstam – 'to all those in the wind, blown through the world like leaves'. In the following poem, 'It Goes On', he addresses Lorca again, this time directly:

> It goes on, Federico, it goes on –
> in the hearts of the functionaries
> who despise the poor they serve ...

Nine Bright Shiners, winner of the 2015 *Irish Times* Poetry Now Award, is split into five parts, with the middle section being named 'Chorus'. This is a nod to Dorgan's awareness of song and traditional verse, but it also alludes to its meaning as a 'Band of singers', because Dorgan joins his voice with a host of other poets, in elegy, in translation, and in homage. Several poems are written in the memory of loved ones, a demanding task for any poet, but one which has been met admirably in poems such as the title poem, and 'Michael, Michael':

> Michael, I was on the East Link in a taxi when the nurse
> in my ear said, soft and sad, I'm afraid your friend is dead.
>
> *A wind out of Munster shook the bridge.*

Compassion, knowledge, and experience lie behind this collection, as they do behind all of those reviewed here. Each one, in its own individual way, displays a genuine sense of what Heaney once referred to as an 'immersion in the craft', and represents a belief in the power and importance of words and music; and of the pursuit of truth, by their means.

Frances Galleymore

STORY

Out of the letter slides a folded page.

           Your hand's so small it struggles
to hold the pencil. Buddleia outside the window.
At our table hatched with scratches
your careful stick-words grow

and from the page fall scarlet walls,
a flag pinned up that's a puzzle to us
but hides cracks.
           A scent of patchouli
in the breath of candlelight, nights
of dance, reviews and screenings,
publisher parties.
           My retreat to our shared den.
Among Gauloises, ink and mugs,
your monkey and girl toys.

           Refolding the page, I notice cars
nose to tail. The houses fat with paint
look up to a sky raked by black
Mickey Mouse ears listening for Sky

and beyond our road the wars are different.

Ian Pople

THE END OF APRIL
  – *in memory of my father*

Finally, at the end of April, when
afternoon light was strong enough
to show the yellow of dandelions,

he might have stroked the leaves
of wild garlic, the thin edges buckling;
he might have touched the underside

of butter burr, the soft hooks that live
out of the light; or ferns, new curlicues
growing among the grey; he might have

felt the crisp feathers of the Canada goose
on the canal, stroked the firm back, pushed
down a little, expecting the sanguine body

of the bird to bob back up like a child's toy
on bath water. Except that, towards the end,
having lost the whorls of finger end,

the knuckle, the bone digit that gripped
the pen, the stub that was his forefinger
became too painful to write with; because

these were fingers that had not escaped, that had
formed together into a shape through which
water and sand flowed with equal measure.

John Wedgwood Clarke

RENOVATION

The chisel stuns the brick and rings the hand.
Clink, relax. Clink, relax. Loose mortar landslides

more and more, the arguments of rain and soot
slumping into the memory of a hearth, bird bones

and black sand. The room releases its breath.
Air sucks at the match. The way is clear between

inside and out. A dove on the chimney pot
broods in the blackened throat, the ear a nest.

David Butler

AND THEN THE SUN BROKE THROUGH

A sea of jade and muscatel; the sky, gun-metal.
Landward, the storm-portending birds, white-lit,
Riding wild contours of wind, uplift
To tilt at the raucous crows. This
Is how it is to live, the ticker tells,
Looping the floor of the newsfeed.
Somewhere, an outrage; an airstrike;
Somewhere, a politic withdrawal. This
Is how it is to live: the wind blowing
The charcoal of crows' feathers;
The rent in the clouds; oblique tines beating
Sudden ochre out of a sullen ocean.

GWYNETH LEWIS IN CONVERSATION WITH COLETTE BRYCE

Gwyneth Lewis writes in both English and Welsh. Her first collection, *Parables & Faxes* (1995), was shortlisted for the Forward Prize and won the Aldeburgh Poetry Festival Prize. *Y Llofrudd Iaith* (2000) won the Welsh Arts Council Book of the Year Prize. Her first non-fiction prose book, *Sunbathing in the Rain: A Cheerful Book about Depression*, was published in 2002. Her recent books include *A Hospital Odyssey* (2010), which takes the form of an epic poem about a journey through illness; and *Sparrow Tree* (2011), shortlisted for the 2012 Wales Book of the Year Award.

Colette Bryce: We're here in the Robinson Library at Newcastle University taking a look at the proofs of your 1995 collection *Parables & Faxes*. Your manuscripts form part of the Bloodaxe Books archive recently acquired by the University. It's now almost twenty years since you would have sent in that manuscript. Can you remember how and why you brought your work to Bloodaxe?

Gwyneth Lewis: I'd met Neil [Astley] at a poetry conference that was run by the WEA in Belfast and he'd invited me to send a manuscript in. I was very grateful to Bloodaxe for giving me the chance from the start, because even then it was difficult to get a first collection published. It's become even more difficult since. But I think that Neil has a talent for spotting up-and-coming people.

CB: Did you feel part of the generation that was forming in those days? There was the big promotion, the New Generation Poets, a couple of years earlier. Were you aware of being part of a generation that was breaking new ground? Stirring things up?

GL: Well, at that time, in the Nineties, there was a lot of nonsense being talked about poetry being the new rock 'n' roll, especially in relation to the New Generation Poets – there was a lot of publicity about poetry. It was always business as usual for the poets. Certainly business as usual for me.

CB: Rock 'n' roll, yes – there were a few leather jackets. That's about as far as it went.

GL: Poetry is the new poetry! That's the point. So, you know, I wasn't part of that promotion so it kind of passed me by. I just wanted to write and get published.

CB: As we're here in an archive context today, I wanted to ask about your writing process and how archival you are in that. Do you keep drafts, for example, do you number or date them?

GL: My paperwork is obsessive. When I'm actually working, I keep everything. The first draft has to be written by hand on paper. And then in order to correct it I print it out and then I keep drafts. My method has changed somewhat. I used to work line by line and I couldn't go on to the second line until the first line was right. So there would be a lot of re-writing by hand. I've changed how I work now. But I still don't throw things out. It's not a question of being archival, but anal! There's a huge amount of stuff lying around. In fact I showed the archivists from the National Library of Wales – which is where my archive has gone – and they were amazed at how neat and chronological it was. From the age of seven to the present day. It's actually made the rafters of the house spring up a bit because there's not quite so much weight!

CB: Going back to the manuscript in front of you, *Parables & Faxes* was your first collection in the English language. I believe you'd published a couple of books in Welsh before that?

GL: Yes. I'd published my first Welsh book in 1990, and a couple of pamphlets earlier. So I'd been through the publication process before, that absolutely wonderful moment when you see the book, see the whites of its eyes. And you think that everything may be alright for a moment until you start getting restless again. But yes, it wasn't my first experience, but it's different because it's a distinct audience. Whereas I knew very well the Welsh language audience, this was completely new territory for me.

CB: Around that time you wrote about the status of the Welsh language: 'Half a million speakers, numbers in decline, it's an all-hands-on-deck situation.' Do you feel the situation for the Welsh language has improved now, fifteen years on from devolution? And by extension, have things improved for Welsh-language authors and poets?

GL: When *Parables & Faxes* was published in 1995, I was asked a lot about being a Welsh-language poet and I think I was quite pessimistic about the future. I remember being in Barcelona with RS Thomas once, and him being asked the same question, and I was more pessimistic than RS was, which was sobering. In fact statistics show that the decline in the language has continued and there are key communities where there's no longer the percentage needed to keep a momentum going socially. So I'm no more hopeful, to be honest with you. And of course poets these days are far more vulnerable to austerity funding-cuts than most kinds of writers. So in some ways things are worse. We have a National Poet of Wales now, a job that didn't exist at the time, and that's good, it's given us a shop front to the world. But on the whole, I think life is harder, not easier, for poets, because reviewing space has shrunk in the broadsheets. I think the profile of poetry is suffering as part of the growing commercialisation of publishing. So there are huge challenges, and we're vulnerable.

CB: Do you feel part of a constituency of bilingual poets? And I'm thinking here about Irish-language poets like Nuala Ní Dhomhnaill and also those who write in Scots Gaelic. How appropriate do you think Ní Dhomhnaill's image of the mermaid is to the condition of the bilingual writer?

GL: It is an unusual situation to be bilingual and publishing in both languages, but I remember being very grateful for a conversation with Nuala Ní Dhomhnaill – we were in Vienna, of all places. She observed that those of her relatives who didn't keep up with their first language had suffered from mental discomfort and illness. And that to me made a lot of sense. So in a way, it's a question of physical health or of physical integrity to use the language that is hard-wired into your brain. I think that her book about the mermaid is a wonderful explanation of the acute discomfort of being in between two cultures, of paying a price to belong to either one. The mermaid who comes from the sea and who goes ashore leaves her own background, but neither is she comfortable at sea. So I think it's a marvellous image, it's a very important book to me that one.

CB: It's so interesting what you say about that conversation. We think also about the idea of repressing art in terms of mental health. It's such an interesting parallel about repressing one's original language.

GL: It is.

CB: I was going to mention RS Thomas, who has already crept into the conversation. I was reading a piece you wrote about him and about your initial difficulties with the kind of nationalism which is implied in some of his early poems. Did wrestling with those issues help you define your own position? Because, later, you became the first National Poet of Wales. Must the Welsh poet take a stand on ideas of nationhood?

GL: It would be very difficult to imagine a Welsh poet – particularly a Welsh-language poet – who didn't have to sort out what he or she thought about her own politics. It's such a beleaguered community that there's little privacy about one's political views. It's an urgent matter because we are talking about a linguistic crisis and a social one as well.

Wales has many of the most deprived areas in Britain. We were brought up reading RS Thomas and his early nationalist poems – you accept them uncritically when you're in school. And then, when I started wanting to be a writer myself I found myself in open revolt against them for all kinds of reasons, not least that you do revolt against your predecessors. I cut my teeth on staking out a position for myself which is different from people like RS Thomas. I think he had difficulties with his early political position, because he abandoned it and then became a great religious poet. I think that was always his poetic vocation. But there is also the sense that whenever I'm told that I have to toe a line I'm perverse, or contrary if you like, and want to look at the other side of the argument. I think every poet should be sceptical as much as possible about language and about those ideas associated with it: 'question everything' is my view.

CB: He was a good model in that respect. You did say in the piece that you went on to become friends in his later years. In fact, in one of the books of yours that I most admire, *A Hospital Odyssey*, there are some words from Thomas woven into the poetry, about Coleridge's notion of fancy and imagination. The quote is 'RS Thomas, I can hear his voice, / told me once that I should choose / between fancy and imagination. / I know it's the latter that I revere.' Could you say a little more about that distinction?

GL: RS Thomas and I did become friends late in his life, well into his eighties, and I've got quite a few letters from him and I treasure them. He was very kind to me. I could write to him about things that worried me as a poet and would always get an answer by return of post. A proper letter. I had been worried about something and he told me to remember always to go for the imagination rather than fancy, in Coleridge's sense of the imagination being the primary faculty of reshaping the world, and fancy being somehow a lesser ... well, it's not quite a faculty in the same way as imagination is, but a lesser skill. However, as I grow older I'm thinking, what would it be like to take fancy as your main principle? I think you would actually get some very interesting poetry from that as well. If he was still here I would be writing to him, saying 'Well, yes, you know, but what about fancy as a god?' Just to make trouble!

CB: It's funny, because you enact it in *A Hospital Odyssey*, you come up with this idea of hell as an airport. And then, in the poem, you reject it as 'fancy'. You say, 'I'm not going to do it.'

GL: Quite often I find that I've written a poem which is adequate and think, 'Oh, that's it.' And then you think 'No, I know there's more to be found underneath that, the ground that poem is on', you know? I have to dig deeper. And I think the fancy is the poem that is good enough for today because I can't bear to think about it any longer. But it doesn't allow you to write out of pain and the access to emotion isn't the same. I think that's one of the main differences.

CB: You did dig deeper in an epic sense in *A Hospital Odyssey*, in following the epic's convention of going into the underworld. Not only the underworld, of course. The poem takes us through the human body, the solar system, the ocean's abyss, to name but a few of the episodes. Can you say a little about the formal vehicle you selected to carry this ambitious narrative, and how you approached plotting on such a scale?

GL: It took me about five years to prepare to write *A Hospital Odyssey*. I've been a fan of epics ever since school. I read Virgil, *loved* Virgil, and Milton. I had wanted to do one forever. So it came directly from the experience of spending a lot of time in hospital with my husband. So rather than go nuts I just kept notes and kept looking and imagining. That, somehow, was enough of a displacement activity to get through the experience of chemotherapy with him. Although, of course, it was he who was ill, not me. I wrote out a plot synopsis before writing the book, thinking 'this will change, it doesn't matter' and in fact it didn't change that much. In epic you have to get the plot right: that's the difference between epic and a lot of other forms. The action is the thing in the epic. So I at least knew enough to get the plot to be credible. If you think that crashing in on a microbes' ball is credible! But on its own terms, you know? It took a lot of time reading and thinking about what I thought health might be, and what words might have to do with health.

CB: It's a wonderful exploration of all of that, but also of the hospital environment and, of course, the state of the National Health Service, which becomes a big part of it.

GL: Yes, it's written by a child of the NHS, and of course with all the problems of hygiene and hospital-acquired infections in mind. How certain basic ways of nursing, perhaps, have been neglected in some places. But it was a tremendously joyful thing to write. It took me nine months from start to finish. Well, nine months and five years! So I was really pleased when Neil liked it and he decided to print it in a trade-sized paperback. The technical measure I adapted from François Villon. He was a medieval French poet of the body, wrote about people in a very realistic way, real people. So I adapted his ballad form and took it for a drive. Hoping that it wouldn't be what Les Murray calls a 'stone jeep'. You know – you just sit in it and it goes nowhere. But this one did take me some distance.

CB: You've spoken about plotting the rhymes always a little way in advance so there was always something to work through.

GL: Yes. What makes epic distinctive is that your narrative is what takes you through the ideas. And it was very interesting to find how narrative and rhyme go at a slightly different pace, and I think the rhymes are coming out of your unconscious, whereas the plot goes more slowly. So I'd always want to go almost faster with the rhymes than the narrative could keep up with.

CB: And does this explain the little digressions that are going on, often chasing the rhymes? You go off on little tangents from the narrative.

GL: I don't know, I mean you can only allow yourself a certain number of digressions because you have to get back to the action, and 'How am I going to get characters into the underworld? Oh, I know, I'll do it through a spider's chamber!'

CB: I wanted to ask you about form, more generally. You've used traditional, and often difficult, forms from the word go in your English-language poetry. In your first book there's a sestina and a villanelle, for example, and very many different stanza forms. And the villanelle appears again in *Sparrow Tree*, your latest book. How does your relationship with traditional form change over the course of a career?

GL: I started off wanting to find out which forms I would enjoy and wanting to try everything. It was like being in the sweet shop, 'Ooh, I'll try that, and that.' And then as I go on I'm less interested in fixed forms and more interested in free verse. Because the traditional forms tend to sound like … a bit like these cardboard boxes [*points to archive boxes nearby*]. You have to be extremely skilful to make them feel organic. So I've been exploring more elusive forms. Although, oddly enough, they're harder and more strict in some ways. You just judge then differently. And then *A Hospital Odyssey,* of course, was a thing on its own. You don't have to rhyme in an epic but I decided to rhyme because I thought it would be easier to keep moving. It did pay off. That form does give you stamina. So it's changing all the time.

CB: You've said, 'I am a formalist, but I think that poetry's content is as – if not more – important than its theatrical effects.' Can you say a little more about content in poetry?

GL: Yes. I was arguing that the whole point of poetry is the content. I'm fascinated by form, but there's no reason for jumping through all these formal hoops unless the content that you present at the end is served by those techniques. Poetry's way of looking at the world is unique. It has a focus and precision that normal perception, which isn't encoded or set into a poem, doesn't possess. It's the difference between looking through binoculars and looking with the naked eye at a bird over there. So it's a question of quality, but it's also a question of coupling your own insights with those in that tradition. You have available to you the sensibilities of more people and better people than yourself, which is one of the reasons it's good quality. So I think it's not talked about enough, content. Because it's difficult to put your finger on it doesn't mean there's no reason to try.

CB: That's true. And talk of content sometimes leads us to questions of autobiography. Subjects that are assumed to reflect the events of a poet's life. You've said, 'The world described in a poem doesn't exist, because the poem itself is the world.' This made perfect sense to me in relation to questions of autobiography. Would you like to share any more thoughts on that idea of content and autobiography?

GL: I think the poems are autobiographical, obviously they are, but not in the way that people think. They expect the biographical details to be the same. Which they're not – not in my poems, anyway. I make things up and put things in code, and so on and so forth. But what we're describing in poems – or what I or what any poet describes in a poem – isn't just a description of life, it is life itself. Because we are all made of the same stuff, we are not separate, you can trace the way in which the world itself behaves like a work of art. And this comes not from a fanciful comparison by me, but from the scientists themselves. So how lucky are we to be working in poetry, which is the universe? So why everybody doesn't think that poetry is as important as science I don't know, but it is a form of science.

CB: In the first of your lecture series for Newcastle University (2014), you referred to depression as being linked to a refusal to do your work as a poet. Poetry, you said, 'is a force to be obeyed. Otherwise it will tear you to pieces'. Would you like to talk about the ways in which we might refuse to do our work as poets, and the consequences?

GL: Yes, in my book *Sunbathing in the Rain* I said that I've noticed that when I get depressed it's very often because I'm refusing to do my proper job, artistically. My job as a poet. Of course, depression occurs for all kinds of reasons and I'm just speaking about myself, but I think if you take poetry as a shorthand for the thing that everybody feels most passionately about – and it may be directed towards potted plants or fishing or whatever – it's that one thing that you feel you were born to do, and that you're most yourself doing.

CB: A calling?

GL: It's a calling, a vocation, and if you refuse that there are consequences. I think that poetry is very difficult and one of the reasons is that there are many ways of dodging this work, but luckily there are forces that keep you to the mark, and for me one of them is depression. So whenever I'm getting hyperactive or getting obsessed with things that are not important I get a warning shot across the bows, 'Oh, just remember what's important'. And this usually means resting more, being more contemplative, you know, living close to the ground, if you like, and writing more. It's no accident that those healthful activities are the same things that allow me to be well and to write.

CB: You quoted Elizabeth Bishop wishing that poets could have a 'self-doubt lobotomy'. What is the role of self-doubt for the poet? Can it ever be a useful thing?

GL: I'd like to put myself on the waiting list for one of Bishop's 'self-doubt lobotomies', but I think, actually, that self-doubt is essential. Because without it, what are we left with? The rampant ego? Well that's no good to anybody. Also I think that radical self-doubt is what makes you a poet, because you don't know where you are in the world therefore you have to frame it, locate yourself in it. It's the only way in which you can make your way forward. I don't see it working for a poet without that self-doubt, I think it's a fundamental position and not to be lobotomized away. It's precious, but it's painful. But then, we're not going in for beauty competitions so perhaps we don't need it, that confidence.

CB: Perhaps it's got a relationship with our inner editor as well, that questions everything we do. Sometimes perhaps too much?

GL: Too much, yes. Ouch.

CB: You've mentioned already your popular book about depression, *Sunbathing in the Rain*, and you've written another prose work about sailing around the world with your husband. Following on, then, how does writing prose affect the health of the poet self? I ask this because Ted Hughes famously attributed a crash in his immune system to too many years writing prose. Do you experience much difference in the processes?

GL: I was aware of the Ted Hughes quote. I don't know what he'd been doing or how his inner economy worked, but I've found prose very interesting. And it's good for me in the sense that you can earn some money doing it. More money than with poetry, of course. But I also find that good poetry has the quality of good prose, in that you're taking your reader with you, there's a logic always in a poem, there's thinking going on. And there are things to be learned from writing prose, so I don't have a difficulty. I think there's a genre incompatibility, perhaps, between fiction and poetry, but I don't find non-fiction at all hostile to poetry. They're very much drawn from the same part of the psyche. I enjoy it and it's also great not to have to worry about the location of every single word in a prose book.

CB: And finally, Gwyneth, what's next for you? In prose or in poetry, what are you working on?

GL: Well, I'm about to put the manuscript in for a novella about being haunted by Dylan Thomas. We're in the centenary year so I've written a facetious novel about living with Dylan Thomas and trying to imagine what that would be like. I'm going to America for a little while to teach. And I'm hoping to publish a collection of Welsh-language poems next year – I'm always working on poems in both languages, actually.

CB: How long has it been since you published a collection of Welsh-language poetry?

GL: I think it's over a decade.

CB: That's exciting.

GL: It is, yes, and terrifying. And also satisfying. I'm looking forward to it. I'm always trying to do the frightening thing, you never can rest on what you've done. It's always going on to the next difficult thing.

This interview took place in March 2014

Libby Hart

HIS COUNTRY IS CALLING ME

And when I say *his country*,
I mean the sweet, sad earth of line and skin. Track of bone, of limb.
His country is calling me.

And when I say *his country*,
I mean that haunt of eyes, cliff of smile. Lea of uncut hair.
I mean that crowded city of heart. His knoll of soul.

I mean blood roar. I mean lush beat.
Each hammer and drum.
Its heat – a chant, a spell.

Enda Coyle-Greene

THAT BLUE TIME

It's the middle of the night, that blue time
disquieted by the phone in the hall,
so I don't move until I have to
turn and face the worry

he has put on the car's back seat
for weeks to bring to work with him,
and carried home again curling
at the edges like an uneaten lunch.

But what he says makes all the sense
of hieroglyphics cut into a cave wall
in Egypt, or an algebraic theorem
ticked correct only because

I'd learnt the formula by heart.
We drive to collect her. She stands
as we are shown into a room that's bare-
bulbed, fizzed with electricity.

While the village on the hill sleeps
on through other people's lives,
she explains how she'd got lost
and would have stayed

lost had the taxi man she'd flagged
decided otherwise. People are kind,
in the main, frangible as glass,
and it is years before

I need to know this.

Killian O'Donnell

GOLDEN BRIDGE

Wrapped in a jacket of midges
he takes in the water

squaring hatch to artificial
dry on his good days

and on his bad just staring
back into the torrent

that is pouring out of him
and is full

of entanglements, judging
its condition against

an ideal depth and clarity
and trying to decide

whether he should push on
or chance a cast.

Emer Fallon

SCATTERBRAIN

This wind has untethered us all.
Just this morning I found the dog floating
a few feet beyond the hall door.
His eyes were white with terror. Later
a hen blew over the garden fence.
It's this wind. It's doing strange things
to the animals, my hair. Yesterday
I went for a walk and came back
all in a heap.
I barely knew myself in the mirror.
I'd swear that wind blew every thought
I've ever had clean out of my head.
Sometimes I actually forget you are dead.
Sometimes I think the wind
just blew you clean away –
clear across Brandon Bay.
'Come back,' I call. 'Come back.'
But of course you never answer.
'How's she looking this morning?' you'd ask.
Well today the bay looks beautiful –
all cruel glitter and jewels. I miss you
when I load the dishwasher. You were always
so bloody particular about where everything went.
I just don't know anymore.
I sometimes forget what the things are called.
And the bed is cold. I use two quilts most nights.

Alice Lyons

WEAR OUT THE DESK WITH RISK AFTER RISK

Frances Leviston, *Disinformation* (Picador Poetry, 2015), £9.99.
Peter Sirr, *The Rooms* (The Gallery Press, 2014), €11.95.

Painter Philip Guston's artistic achievement is built on his late works which, in their time, were scandalously strange and alienating. Guston remains one of the best examples in living memory of an artist with creative and moral courage who risked much to follow inclinations that were peculiar, unfashionable and contradictory. In the decade before he died, Guston continued to do the abstract, airy drawings and paintings that were in keeping with his hitherto 'signature' work. Yet he also wanted to draw 'real' things, a pursuit anathema to any card-carrying member of New York's Abstract Expressionists. Nevertheless, Guston ploughed on and made countless pictures of ordinary stuff: hobnailed boots, lightbulbs, overflowing ashtrays, junk. He became unwilling to relinquish either inclination in the pursuit of the 'coherent', a quality too often prized for its ready intelligibility to the market rather than its creative octane. Guston's tenacious hold on two reins of contradictory inquiry led to the flowering of those wonderful late works that are still awkward and magnificent, still *sui generis*, still never completely graspable.

The two poets reviewed here, Frances Leviston and Peter Sirr, call the late Guston story to mind. Both are undoubtedly writing out of certain poetic groundings and trajectories that are simple – and tiresome –enough to chart. Yet it is the risk-taking impulses in both that distinguishes them, a sense that both writers are responding to urgent, unpredictable creative promptings beyond their ken. Both have written fresh, exemplary books, inoculations against complacent poetry.

'I am making jelly', begins the title poem of Frances Leviston's *Disinformation*, her second collection. It's the right line to start off this book. Jelly-making is a messy business – gelatin being the product of boiled bones – and so, implies this poet, should be poetry-making. Leviston uses crafted poetic language to put the flesh back on the bones of a world being stripped away by multiple forces of disinformation, which often comes in disembodied form, *e.g.*, guff spewing from radio news; the modern pursuit of the elusive 'lifestyle'; the disappearance of feminine wisdom and power in the modern world.

Disinformation consists of thirty poems in three ten-poem sections. Throughout the book Leviston's gaze is drawn to particularity; the first and third sections abound with still lifes of various oddities, things having a very specific gravity: an IUD, a Parma violet, Lametta (the name for lead

Christmas tinsel – who knew?), memory foam. Leviston steers her poetry close to the texture of the actual, the contours and fractal ins and outs of her chosen objects, as if a poetry that looses itself into such gnarled crannies might get closer to actual 'information'. Or at least be heading in the right direction.

The poem 'GPS' is a portrait of a machine notorious for its monotone misdirection. Leviston's language here is deliciously evocative:

> Like a wet dream this snow-globe was a gift
> to myself. She rides shotgun
>
> or stuck to the dashboard, swirling and swirling
> across the carpet of potholes to my house.
>
> Mantelpiece matryoshka
> she wears an inscrutable face:
>
> there's no telling how many dolls deep she goes
> beyond her one red peanut-shell …

But beyond the elaborate, imaginative portraiture, Leviston is more interested in what happens when the driver throws a monkey-wrench into the GPS mindset by pulling a U-turn. She apostrophizes to the device:

> Her compass boggles. Lie down there in that drift,
> little girl, you're feeling strangely warm,
>
> and something big is about to make sense
> if we just keep going in the opposite direction.

The 'something big' that happens in *Disinformation* arises from its specificity as much as from its U-turns. These strategies read as an ethic, as a countervailing force against the many guises of disinformation including untruth, misdirection or silence. *Disinformation*'s central section, a series of poems in which the wisdom of the goddesses of antiquity are both 'resisting capture' and dissolving in the contemporary world is as serious a feminist critique as Adrienne Rich's early, wonderful *Diving into the Wreck*. In the meditative sequence 'Athenaeum', the speaker implores Minerva to 'guard our sororities that know / no better; shed blessings as we pass / gossiping through the metal-detector doors / on campus, pillars of books / from reading lists / piled against our chests'. Yet the poem makes clear that Minerva's legacy remains an obscure 'palimpsest' within modern academe as obscure as her shrine, what little remains, now part of a National Trust park in 'Edgar's Field, in Handbridge, in Chester'.

A poet writing this close-up and sly has to have Bishop and Moore in the backstory, and 'Bishop in Louisiana' sets that poet in a diluvial landscape. Leviston's diction is finely controlled and, when she takes prudent leaps of register, the language is appropriately enlivened and un-Bishop-like, *e.g.*, the first line of 'Lametta', a cracker of a poem, which reads: 'Fuck me I love the stuff'. About these poems I'd have to say the same thing.

A challenge: how to write a review of Peter Sirr's poetry without using the word 'European'? Or perhaps more seriously, why are 'Continental' and 'European' the default critical adjectives for defining this poet?

An experiment: for 'European' let us plug in the word 'voracious' while reading *The Rooms*. For it becomes quickly apparent that this book gobbles texts and voices from, yes, that continental mass adjacent to this island. But as Sirr puts it toward the end of the collection, 'No writer is an island, / least of all me. / I open my mouth and dozens fall out'. Indeed. *The Rooms* is built not upon the old island/continent dialectic, but on a vast landscape of open mouths that both hunger and give voice. A sensual appetite for world and language, a desire to burst the confines of place and self, permeates these poems. The opening poem, 'The Mapmaker's Song' couldn't state it more clearly: our mapmaker has reached the limit of what his tools can fix:

> I want to be,
> beyond everything I've reached or drawn,
> not much at all, or all there is
> a geographer of breath
>
> a curator of hands.
> I want to lie in the atrium
> of the museum of the fingertip
> and touch, touch, touch.

The central sequence of thirty-four poems, 'The Rooms', enacts these longings in startling, evocative ways. Sirr achieves quite a technical feat; these poems feel at once highly personal and located *and* wholly impersonal and dislocated – as if he wrote his own version of the Glanmore Sonnets and then blew them open with a powerful wind machine. The rooms in 'The Rooms' are porous, barely-there containers for a flurry of unpindownable ghosts, memories and weathers that estrange as much as familiarize:

> … We'll lean, unsteady,
> against a countertop and see
> that everything that matters has gone ahead

> or stand helplessly, flailing at the tide,
> as someone we love tries to put the key in the door
> and tries again, and looks back, unhoused,
> at the sudden strangeness of everything there.

There is a deft balancing in the sequence of glancing, telling detail ('in my arms a heartbreak of laundry'; 'Country music / haunts the rusted Escort'; 'the ants of Tritonville Avenue still organised'), with images and actions that serve to unsettle, disrupt, and overturn. An authentic quality of consciousness and memory is the result, a faithful depiction of how human spaces/rooms/stanzas can hold the tang of past, present and future in one dizzying apprehension.

A less venturesome poet would have settled on that sequence, bookended it with a few poems and left *The Rooms* at that. But then Peter Sirr goes and writes 'An Audience with BB', a multi-vocal, heavily citational sequence that spans twenty-five pages, a poem whose *ars poetica* could be 'fly to the cursor, curl up in paper, / wear out the desk with risk after risk'.

The BB is Bertolt Brecht, and the sequence shifts voice from Brecht's own – snippets of Brecht's poems are collaged throughout the sequence – to a voice from presumably the present addressing Brecht. In a sense, 'An Audience with BB' is yet another iteration of 'The Rooms' in how Sirr braces the 'personal' (the narrator's non-Brecht voice) against the impersonal (Brecht's texts, the Other). Yet it's also a way for this poet to wrangle with larger questions of a poet's agency in troubled times:

> I wasn't alone. In dark times
> no poet is at home. Besides,
> where did Homer live, or Dante?
> Not to mention Li Po and Tu Fu
> shuffling through the war zones
> where millions died.

The quotational format also allows Sirr to entertain 'thoughts' that would never be worded as crudely had he penned them himself. Brecht can veer into melodrama – 'My young son asks me / should I study maths? / What for I want to say. / That two hunks of bread / are more than one / you'll find out soon enough'. But that is the risk. He is also the 'insatiable playwright' whose actors wash off the 'stink of mimicry and stale rhetoric' with 'make up and sweat'. Sirr has chosen an urgent intelligence from the past with which to ventriloquize and ventilate his fine book.

Simon Ó Faoláin

ZEITGEIST

Sinne atá suas
i láthair na huaire,
Ní bhfaighimidne
ár mbás choíche.

Diúltaím don dtaithí,
diúltaím don gcuimhne,
Luím go lán-mhuiníneach
idir basa na heolaíochta,

D'fhonn surfála trén saol
ar feadh síoraíochta
lem' chlár ar chúr
ar bharr an chlog-chuair

Gan *wipeout* go brách,
fiú an *wipeout* mór.

Ceaití Ní Bheildiúin

MATAMAITIC DO SHIANSA ÁR N-ANAMA

CAOINEADH

deor

deor

deor

deora

CAOINEADH AG DUL I LÉIG

ar deoraíocht
deoraí
deora
deor
deo
de´

CUISLE NA MAIDNE

braon
braon drúchta
braon drúchta

braon
braon drúchta
braon draíochta

SEANRITHIM

bualadh
bualadh
bualadh shoc na hinneonach

bualadh
bualadh
bualadh shoc na hinneonach

FORAS

cloch
ar dhá chloch
dhá chloch
ar chloch

Ceaití Ní Bheildiúin

TAR AGUS TÓG

Labhrann an Cnoc:

Má tá cosaint uait, tar
i dtreo mo shleasa is mo dhúnta;
má tá beannacht uait, tar
chun mo thoibreacha;
má tá ort dul i bhfolach, tar
faoi ionarbhréid mo cheo.

Feairim fáilte roimis glaine croí
roimis aigne leathan oscailte.
Altaím taithí nua, cuairteoirí nua -
na laochanna is an lag araon.
Tar ón Afraic is ón Oirthear
ó Siria, ón Eiritré, ón Afganastáin.

Tá scóip anseo ar mo sciortaí
togha is rogha do thithe:
tithe móra an Tíogair Cheiltigh
tithe móra na gcroíthe móra
tithe beaga fáilteacha
tithe lán
ach slí i gcónaí do dhaoine breise iontu
tithe samhraidh, tithe samhlaithe
tithe folmha, tithe ullmha
tithe tréigthe, tithe titithe
tithe tinteáin le ceol is brí
tithe an dua, tithe na sí.

Tar thar lear, thar tairseach chugam –
tá clocháin is botháin
is láithreacha agam
is fothain anseo do phobal.
Tar isteach i mo bharróg.
Tar agus tóg.

Paddy Bushe

A MAJOR VOICE

Cathal Ó Searcaigh, *Aimsir Ársa* (Arlen House, 2013), €15.
Cathal Ó Searcaigh, *An Bhé Ghlas* (Leabhar Breac, 2015), €15.

Some time ago, while I was visiting the Musée d'Orsay, I stopped in amazement at a relief-panel sculpture in mahogany by the nineteenth century French artist Georges Lacombe. Entitled *Isis*, the piece shows a female nude figure, her breasts pouring what might be blood onto the roots of a rampant growth of flowers, her long tresses metamorphosing into the roots and branches of the trees above, trees that stretch away in a colonnade towards a dark green background. Her eyes are closed as if she is in a trance. Her pubic hair seems to blossom on a stalk that is really the thin line between her legs, running up between the cascades from the nipples out of which she is squeezing the life-giving flow. The whole panel, its colours shading from brown to red, is full of fecundity, of sexuality, of the integration of the human with the natural world and especially of the fundamentally feminine nature of all that growth and fertility. I realized I was looking at an earth-goddess, a *Cailleach* as Gearóid Ó Crualaoich has so well established her in the Gaelic world. It is an extraordinarily powerful piece.

But it wasn't just the work itself that had amazed me. Some weeks before that, I had been reading (and translating) Cathal Ó Searcaigh's poem 'An Bhé Ghlas'. It struck me very strongly that Lacombe's sculpture and Ó Searcaigh's poem could have been created as illustrations one of the other. It is worthwhile to google Lacombe's sculpture, to compare with Ó Searcaigh's poem:

> Mise cailleach na coilleadh glaise,
> baineannach craobhfholtach na feise;
>
> (I am the earthwoman of the greenwood,
> the wanton one, leaves in my hair.)

Or, even more startling:

> an ballán cíche i mbarr féithe,
> an cocán róis ag foscladh a ghné,
> raicleach na gcaor, baineannach na gcraobh,
> an chailleach a chuireann
> driuch craicinn ar na firéin.

(the nipple swelling out from the vein,
the rosebud opening its display,
brazen amidst berries, wanton among branches,
the earthwoman who raises
gooseflesh on the faithful.)

The echoes were overwhelming. I asked Cathal at the time if he had ever seen Lacombe's piece. He hadn't. I give space to this only to emphasize what I think is essential in Ó Searcaigh's recent work, as is wonderfully manifest in these two books. He is tapping – in the literal sense – into deep archetypal, communal and individual sources, and the poetry is correspondingly rich and deep. It is fitting and timely that both of these books, published within two years of each other, have received the Oireachtas prize. They are the voice of a major contemporary Irish poet, however marginalized that voice may currently be in the public consciousness.

The poet has been well served by his publishers: Arlen House, noted for its fine productions, has integrated lovely and apposite drawings by Ian Joyce into *Aimsir Ársa*, and Leabhar Breac has presented *An Bhé Ghlas* in fitting garments. Ó Searcaigh's probing of his sources is primarily local, familial and communal. As always, Earagal, wonderfully visible from his house, is essential. And it is essential, not only in a personal sense, but also in a communal, human sense. As well as his own personal engagements, Ó Searcaigh interrogates the mountain from the point of view of his own people:

An cuimhneach leat
na glúnta urramacha
a chaith a mbeatha
ag saothrú is ag síolrú
i dtrath is in antráth
anseo faoi do scáth?

(Do you remember
those venerated generations
who spent their lives
slaving and seeding
in good times and bad
under your shadow?)

The sequence 'Na Bailte Bánaithe' is an elegiac celebration of Ó Searcaigh's own background, a piece that makes pure poetry of acute sociological insight:

Le gach anál dá dtarraingim
motháim iad ag éirí ina nduine
is ina nduine as mínte m'aigne

as na bailte fearainn atá curtha
i bhfód beo mo chuimhne
as cúig ghlúin an dúchais

a thig chun solais anois
is mé ag gabháil i bhfód ionam féin
i mbéal an uaignis

(With every breath I take
I feel them rise up one
after another from the meadowlands of my mind,

from the townlands that are buried
in the living sod of my memory,
from the five generations of *dúchas*

that are coming to light
as I enter into the sod of myself
between the jaws of loneliness.)

This sequence invites comparison with Somhairle MacGill-Eain's masterpiece 'Hallaig', a comparison which I think the greatest Gaelic poet of recent times would not refuse. I believe it to be a work that should be read by not only readers of poetry, but by anyone who is concerned about the future of rural Ireland, Gaelic Ireland, marginalized Ireland.

If Ó Searcaigh digs deep, he also digs wide. Arabic poetry, the poetry of Li Bai, innumerable references to the Gaelic song tradition, these and other sources are all part of his poetic context. A particular favourite of mine invokes the imaginary response of Ovid in relation to the woman who betrayed him under the guise of friendship.

Tá a meáchan féin d'olc
á iompar aici le fada.
Mar chloch, titfidh sí
i bpoll a caillte, slogfar í
sa tsruth guairneáin
a chothaigh si go diabhlaí.
San uisce faoi thalamh
ar a mbeathaíonn sí, báfar í.

> (She has for a long time borne
> the weight of her own malice.
> Like stone, she will drop
> down her abyss of loss, will be swallowed
> in the whirlpools
> she has malevolently stirred.
> In the subterranean cauldrons
> that nurture her, she will drown.)

Ó Searcaigh, as this extract shows, has a sharp ear for the contemporary, even the personal resonance of a classical or historical theme. This shows itself in other poems, poems where classical Arabic poetry is invoked in an imaginative integration with young gay men caught up in war and also as victims of a homophobic culture. It is caught also in a fine poem celebrating an uncle who fought in WWI. Almost always, the poems are brought home from their historical or literary setting to the poet's own life and experience, and they create a correspondingly rich resonance. Even Roger Casement turns up in Donegal, in an erotic context that will probably not be celebrated over the next few centennial months. Ó Searcaigh's intelligent, mischievous and provocative voice has not been silenced.

In *Aimsir Ársa*, Ó Searcaigh invoked Li Bai, the great classical Tang Chinese poet. In *An Bhé Ghlas*, some of the titles could have been stolen from the same poet. 'Tá na Lilí i mBláth ar an Dúloch' is a lovely rhythmic evocation of what Ó Searcaigh calls 'loiteog na gréine ionam / the lotus of the sun in me', an orientalization of where he lives, or a homecoming from where he has been. I think it is this domestication of Ó Searcaigh's poetic wanderings that has enormously energized his most recent work. The domestic and the foreign have wonderfully enhanced one another. In 'Tá na Lilí i mBláth ar an Dúloch' (the title itself a poem), Ó Searcaigh gives a 'whoop of joy' as he contemplates the lilies in the Dúloch lake:

> Ansiúd ag aoibhniú na locha
>   sa chruth is go ligim
>   liú áthais asam ...

The coinage of 'ag aoibhniú na locha' is wonderful, as is the contemplation of the lilies in the face of

> I ndiaidh a raibh de mhéala
>   ag cur mairge orm
>   i gcaitheamh na bliana.

The contemplative note of oriental poetry is made domestic here, in a credible and relevant way. Ó Searcaigh has a lot to say, and says it wonderfully.

There is a deep and intense integrity which is central to Ó Searcaigh's work. As he so often says himself, 'an teanga' is what is central to his poetry. His affirmation of, and celebration of, his own language and background, with their attendant values, is as genuine as his questioning of some of those values when they become oppressive. And however critical he may sometimes be, he never hides behind the ironic, or the mask of self-protection. He bares his linguistic, cultural and poetic soul in a way that can be easily mocked or dismissed by those who shy away from honesty and plain speaking. However much that this has been exploited, let us give thanks for a poet of such values, and for the poetry that ensues.

Mary Melvin Geoghegan

THE RAIN AT THE WINDOW

is bursting to get in.
I think I'll open the window
see where it wanders
give it the run of the house
upstairs, between the sheets.

Nerys Williams

BIBLIOPHILE
  – after Wim Wenders

When I think like a child
I become the child.

Though my flight absconds
from a divided city,

with its time of questions
its susurrus of a library.

Voices grow to a choir
of utterance in my head.

When the child was a child
sunlight was slight,

and spots of rain
were marvels.

The flower imagined
folding into nightfall.

Evil did not exist
except in battered books.

A man looks over his shoulder
stares into space and whispers:

'I want the now and now and now
to follow the incline of her neck.'

Weighted against the consolation of angels
who brush against the hurt of ordinary lives.

Who tell us the dear one is asleep in the next room.
Who tell us to testify is never enough.

Patrick Deeley

POULTICE

A moth pinches and presses itself in under the glass lampshade
fixed to my hotel-room ceiling, where it clicks and flutters
all evening, singed and stunned and flaring again out of its dying
to fret and flounder in the light. I watch the fool's gold
of its wings collect as in a Petri dish above my head, and feel
how far I fall short of my wish-fulfilment. And miss
the self-abandon of the hurt boy delving fingers into wild hives
for solace not of honey but of bee stings, or sleeping
under the rough mercy of furze, or jumping from trees, or diving
in wells to cool the ardour of nettles, pismires, sunburn.
And miss a mad boy's seeming intention to maim himself before
the sometime kindness of the earth became his own.
Arc of hare, lift of lark, the marsh fritillary's flit-with-breezes,
each Callows river meandering to loops that gathered the waders –
long-shanked, long-billed – in little picture-book lakes.
No soft sentiment, no cure but make do with slow mending.
So I haul up from nature's messy heaven this poultice that resolves
to a tingle, an afterglow, a turning page – cornucopia
of images, metaphor and onomatopoeia huffed off a spot-lit stage.

Aidan Rooney

IN A COUNTRY CHURCHYARD

We want him to go out on a high note,
said the gravedigger's eldest son, himself
a gravedigger. He stood back from the edge,
his right foot on the left lug of a spade.
White orchids dressed the rug of man-made grass
rolled out over planks laid across the space.

His father sat fornenst the opened plot
on a stone wall the sun going down lit up.
It shone on the flowers and warmed the father,
his good cap doffed, his head inclined in rest.
He'd dug for everyone in the graveyard,
Mad Dog even, and the Hunger Strikers.

We haven't told him yet, the son disclosed,
but will when all the fuss is over.
His father's hair, as the poet's used to, glowed
in a sudden, sideways burst of sunshine.
Magnesium burning. And would not let up
no matter the light. Or the light dying.

After tea, the son drove in the digger,
its link-box raised, then tipped, to fill the hole
with shingle from the shoreline of Lough Neagh.
It fell like the wall of a waterfall.
He watched his father through its thinning veil
get up to get the shovel and the rake.

Caitríona O'Reilly

A KIND, COLD EYE

Dennis O'Driscoll, *The Outnumbered Poet: Critical and Autobiographical Essays* (The Gallery Press, 2013), €17.50.
Dennis O'Driscoll, *Update: Poems 2011-2012* (Anvil Press, 2014), £8.95.

Dennis O'Driscoll's sudden death in 2012 robbed the Irish literary landscape of one of its most clear-sighted and erudite poet-critics. *The Outnumbered Poet* is a sizeable collection of his critical and auto/biographical writings and a successor to his acclaimed prose collection *Troubled Thoughts, Majestic Dreams* (2001). As a critic O'Driscoll is never soft, but he is always fair, and his conclusions are grounded in a balanced assessment of the text and a judicious weighing in the scale with his wide-ranging knowledge. In several essays he casts an amused eye on the depredations of contemporary 'PoBiz', upon which he is hilariously excoriating – inveighing against what he calls 'blurbonic plague', for instance – but as usual, he has a serious point to make:

> Two doting blurbists, enlisted like godparents at a baptism or sponsors at a confirmation, are far less valuable to poets and readers than two disinterested critics. How many of the hundreds of new collections are adequately evaluated before being swept away as the next year's newborn volumes, each swaddled in its christening robe of embroidered blurbs, are delivered?

O'Driscoll is of Yeats's view that 'none of us can say who will succeed, or even who has or has not talent. The only thing certain about us is that we are too many.' It is sobering to think that Yeats claimed to have said this at the Rhymer's Club in the 1890s after a particularly crowded session (and one wonders whether he had been reading Hardy); proof perhaps that despite what we may think to the contrary, poetic overpopulation is not a new phenomenon. The title essay, delivered as an address to the Poetry Now Festival in Dún Laoghaire in 2003, is a witty but pointed examination of the culture of poetry readings. O'Driscoll asks:

> [W]hy do genuinely talented poets dissipate so much unrenewable energy on readings and reading tours, instead of remaining within productive reach of their desks?

His speculations on the reason for this extend from examinations of the performance instinct and George Mackay Brown's imagined medieval

Orkney balladeers, via caustic remarks on the subject by Juvenal and Martial, to contemporary poets who fall into two camps: 'those who cannot be persuaded to step up to the reading podium and those who cannot be coaxed down'. He is scathing on the latter: 'indefatigable stentorians who travel about like missionaries, taking their work to wherever two or three have gathered in poetry's name'. As usual, O'Driscoll is discreet, but he has considerable fun describing the backstage bitch-slapping he once witnessed as two poets jockeyed for reading priority, or describing Richard Murphy's very funny account of his reading with James Dickey, who swore 'that he was not going to be a curtain-raiser for any goddamn unknown Irish poet'. That word 'indefatigable' could be applied to O'Driscoll himself with a more positive valence; despite his identification of these follies, these fallings away from the ethical and aesthetic ideal, there is no jadedness, never a sense that true poetry, that elusive gleam of gold in the alluvium, is something he ever tired of seeking out.

Among many riches in this collection, the more personal essays about O'Driscoll's own development as a young poet are the most moving. The wonderful essay 'The Library of Adventure' charts the beginnings of the bibliophile's mania: 'whatever had been written, I wanted to read. Whatever there was to read, I wanted to have read. Eventually, what there wasn't to read, I wanted to write': one surmises that this instinct never left him. His eidetic recall is remarkable in this and other pieces; as an essayist he has an uncanny ability to conjure up a vanished era, whether it is the Thurles of the early 1960s and an image of himself as a book-obsessed child reading 'in a large tea chest propped against the smooth bark of a mature laburnum tree', or the ambiance of mid-Eighties literary Dublin in his long essay about Michael Hartnett. The city and its literary atmosphere have changed so much in the decades since, and O'Driscoll's fidelity to its memory is so striking and so evocative that it is not an overstatement to say that these essays are important acts of recuperation and witness in their own right, destined to become a part of the city's perpetual self-inscription.

The Michael Hartnett essay is in many respects the centrepiece of the book, constituting as it does a major, and likely definitive, reappraisal of the poet's work. This far-reaching and detailed critical assessment is movingly bookended by O'Driscoll's personal recollections of his encounters with the poet: ' "Heine is so sad," Hartnett sighed to me once; and, contemplating his meagre frame, as he diced fatalistically with alcoholic death, I knew what Lorca meant when he said "the duende does not come at all unless he sees that death is possible." ' O'Driscoll, with customary perspicacity and critical patience, gives Hartnett his full due, recognizing his extravagant gifts but not soft-pedalling on his flaws either, chief among which was the quixotic and ultimately self-defeating 'farewell to English' in 1975. Those of us who might be puzzled by this gesture are given an insight, in the course of this sensitive essay, into the conflicting necessities that drove Hartnett:

> [N]o language is 'foreign' to the poet who makes it his own, as Hartnett – a native speaker of English, after all – had ably done before entering the dyspeptic, opinionated phase of which 'A Farewell' is a prime specimen. But no poet can be entirely at ease with his or her language; bridging the gap between impulse and expression, between what is imagined and what can be verbalized, is the nub of the artistic process. The waning of Hartnett's inspiration and intensity levels may have caused him to mistake an artistic crisis (or even a 'middle-age crisis' of confidence) for a linguistic one. In the end he was no more at home in Irish than in English [...] – less so, if anything.

O'Driscoll is just as insightful about Hartnett's Irish language work as he is about the poetry in English. He praises 'Inchicore Haiku', 'a limpid, chastened sequence, composed in the most concise and pinched of forms', but is less convinced of the merits of 'Sibelius in Silence', Hartnett's last significant poem, disagreeing with Paul Durcan's assessment of it as a major work; although O'Driscoll's issue with the poem seems to be as much a queasiness about its perceived politics of 'mystical nationalism' than about its artistic merits per se. *The Outnumbered Poet* concludes with three essays on Seamus Heaney: a study of Heaney's *Electric Light* from 2006, a review of the Michael J Durkan / Rand Brandes *Seamus Heaney: A Bibliography 1959-2003*, and a consideration of Heaney as public poet. As a critic of Heaney, O'Driscoll is remarkable: encyclopaedically knowledgeable, inexhaustible, penetrating and perhaps erring only very occasionally on the side of awe.

More than anything, though, this collection of essays lives in the vividness of its vignettes: the Old Testament prophet-figure of RS Thomas with his 'jeremiad against contemporary poetry' enjoying a surprisingly convivial evening with Czesław Miłosz at the Shelbourne Hotel – much to O'Driscoll's delight and relief, having engineered the meeting himself; several Dublin meetings with a bibulous, rebarbative and eccentrically dressed Miroslav Holub; recollections of a scintillating Robert Lowell reading at Kilkenny Arts Week in 1975.

Update: Poems 2011-12 comprises thirty-three poems that were found on a file on Dennis O'Driscoll's computer after his death, and the book reproduces his file exactly as he left it. The poems are full of O'Driscoll's customary disabused wit but there is a darkened vision here also, loath as one is to impose a retrospective teleology upon them:

> We have worked through most of life's
> set-pieces now, assumed the roles of mewling
> infant, truant student, canteen-fed breadwinner,
> toothless, treble-voiced old codger.
>
> Our 'exeunt all' phase is advancing ...
> – 'COMEDY'

Poems such as 'Then' or 'The Main Event' are shadowed by a melancholy but resigned presentiment, but there is humour in this collection too, albeit of a mordant kind. O'Driscoll is politically scathing in 'Ticking the Boxes' and the prose poem 'Or Bust', a virtuosic riff on the kind of focus-grouped doublespeak politicians specialize in:

> Learn to say you fell victim to a global downturn, stiff competition from the East, soaring labour costs, crippling taxation, unfavourable exchange rates, excessive regulation and compliance requirements – red tape gone mad – not to mention insufficient vigilance of cowboy operators, cack-handed official crackdowns on the black economy.

Given his civil service career, O'Driscoll has always written with a finely-tuned ear and a wickedly humorous tone on linguistic enormities of the kind perpetrated by politicians and PR men, and the poems in *Update* are no exception. Yet the darkness underneath the wit is never far away. Several of the poems examine with great honesty and poignancy a nostalgia for the certainties and reassurances of faith, most notably the title poem, which casts the speaker in the role of spurned lover: 'What a good listener you always were / to me, God. I so wish we had not quarrelled, / gone our separate ways.' Like Philip Larkin, O'Driscoll is not one for easy consolation, and the vision in these poems remains clear-eyed and uncomfortably stark. If the essays gathered in *The Outnumbered Poet* are striking for their vivid recollection of detail, much the same quality is evident in this collection, and it is in such detail that comfort and continuity are to be found. The lovely and moving poem with which this short collection ends, 'Bedtime,' depicts the poet's uncle in a rural setting 'plotting his tomorrows before sleep', and opens to an undimmed vision of loving recall:

> Day's over-eager light does not know when
> to stop: I can still speedread wallpaper rosebuds,
> bear witness to the holy pictures' apparition.
>
> A Beauty of Bath apple ferment overwhelms
> the back room, where pheasants slump from
> doors in autumn, and vital supplies are stored:

>   plump beer-bellied Guinness bottles and Time ale
>   for visitors; Corcoran's orangeade; selection boxes
>   of Lemon's Pure Sweets for grandchildren ...

The poems in this volume may not comprise a full collection, and one can only speculate unusefully about how O'Driscoll might have wished to alter or add to them, but they are a welcome addition to the dazzling, and now sadly complete, oeuvre by means of which Dennis O'Driscoll greatly enriched the literary culture of his time.

Joanna Guthrie

SMALL HOURS

An owly night
with a curl of moon like ginger-peel.

At the cottage near the river's source
I stick my head out:
the sky has shaken itself clear with cold.
The old puzzle covers the ceiling above the thatch,
dizzy with stars nodding their heads
and saying: it is what you think it is.
It's over. It won't finish.
Go back to bed.

Niamh Flanagan

Haystacks, Cill Rialaig
Etching, 10 cm x 10 cm

www.niamhflanagan.com

Niamh Flanagan

Hidden Trophy
Etching, 20 cm x 20 cm

www.niamhflanagan.com

Niamh Flanagan

Sheep Island – there was no boat
Etching, 10 cm x 10 cm

www.niamhflanagan.com

Niamh Flanagan

Things we've lost, things we've found
Etching, 20 cm x 20 cm

www.niamhflanagan.com

John Murphy

BIRD

Do me a favour: shut up about your father.
Mine's twenty years dead, give or take
a week or two. And, no, I can't find my mother.
But I look for her. I do. Nights I walk

the borders of the past, listening for a one-note bird,
for the brassy clap-trap of crows on the roof,
for a voice heard only in sleep, a word
in a dream. And when I sleep she speaks

through years long overgrown, through vines
that choke the light from one good day. It's July.
I'm eight years old. Neil Armstrong has yet to fluff his lines.
Look, she says, embracing a moon I'll never see again.

Her arms unfold like wings – she leaves too soon.
She leaves a trapped absence in the eaves of my room.

Tom French

NORTH OF THE VILLAGE

He would live on the clippings of tin,
and if he gave the last of a lambing away,
time after time, think no less of him,

for this was good husbandry,
and strong twins fetched a sight more
than a middling threesome at Ardee Fair.

There is a mowing bar propped in a corner
under a portrait of St Martin de Porres,
a bearing still in the plastic he bought it in,

parts of the briar pipes he smoked
kept in a biscuit tin in the hopes
of making one decent one,

the insides of carbide lamps
from a life lived in a blackout;
his bed, its wrought iron ends,

as much a machine as the mangle
and the dung spreader manacled
by brambles in the haggard.

The stone path he took to the village
is a strip of high ground now
where spring grass gets it hard to grow.

There is where he dammed the water to wash;
his scythe hangs where he kept it in the thatch.
Birds are plundering the horse's collar

for nesting material, and the handful
of things he hung to dry at the fire
are there yet, dry as a bone.

Out the back pegs survive on a line
tied between trees groaning under fruit.
His damsons are as ripe today as they will ever be.

Tom French

OWENDUFF

> '*glór na habhann, the noise of the river*'
> – *Foclóir Gaedhilge agus Béarla*,
>   edited by Reverend Patrick S Dineen, 1927

The silence I heard
on that last day
will stay with me,

when the fall
at the weir was met
by a rise of the sea,

and the uncommitted,
dry one who
waited for days

for the sun to swim,
believed all that
the ones, pausing

in midstream
from stroking to get
their bearings, said.

Henri Cole

POETA MIRABILIS

Seamus Heaney, *New Selected Poems: 1966-1987* (Faber and Faber 2014), £18.99.
Seamus Heaney, *New Selected Poems: 1988-2013* (Faber and Faber 2014), £18.99.

When Seamus Heaney began writing in his mid-twenties, it was as if he'd taken the lid off an old tobacco tin (his image), whose vacuum seal gave a little sigh and emitted a fragrance that transported him straight back into the whitewashed, thatched one-story house of his childhood. There was a stable for animals located under the same roof that sheltered him and his eight siblings, one of whom, at three and a half, would be struck by a car and die. In 'Mid-Term Break', a solemn poem of adolescence, Heaney remembers: 'I was the eldest, / Away at school, as my mother held my hand // In hers and coughed out angry tearless sighs'. Around the farm house there were dark alders, a garden, and a field with horses. People went to the well for water. It was a secure home without menace, except for the sound of small wild things on the ceiling at night and a child's fecund imagination. Heaney's poems can take the brunt of many things, and his first memory-based poems take the brunt of childhood, a time of 'mud grenades', of 'rat-grey fungus' on fermenting blackberries, and of a 'poppy bruise' on his small brother's left temple after 'the bumper knocked him clear'.

But religion touches everything in the social life of this community, so there is also an awareness of the divisions and a sense of difference, even in a house without sectarian energy. And Heaney eventually also wrote poems that take the brunt of Ireland's difficult history, portraying the experiences of a segregated Catholic minority living in a place that regarded it as an endangering element. These poems' sympathies tilt toward 'the underground man', whose daily existence included tanks, posted soldiers, and other degradations, as in 'Whatever You Say Say Nothing', in which Heaney writes: 'A bomb had left a crater of fresh clay / In the roadside, and over in the trees // Machine-gun posts defined a real stockade.' In 1970, Heaney returned from teaching in the balmy, open atmosphere of Berkeley to the 'meaner exactitudes' of Northern Ireland, where the Provisional IRA had begun its bombing campaign. He said that, until this time, his poems had had 'a stillness' in them as they gazed in a trance at something. But 'Whatever You Say' takes off from a phrase his mother used and plays with the colloquial and evasive remarks that kept people from revealing what they really felt, because their public rhetoric was much more careful than their private sorrows and yearnings.

The poems Heaney wrote during the Troubles are not merely occasional; instead, 'a man's inner energy takes the measure of his outer circumstances and is not oppressed', as he said about Yeats. In 'Whatever You Say', Heaney explains: 'Yet I live here, I live here too, I sing, // Expertly civil tongued with civil neighbours'. To contextualize the violence, he also wrote poems refracting the Irish experience through images of sacrificed bodies of Iron Age men found preserved in bogs, where 'The ground itself is kind, black butter // Melting and opening underfoot' ('Bogland'). In 'The Grauballe Man', Heaney writes of the corpse:

> I first saw his twisted face
>
> in a photograph,
> a head and shoulder
> out of the peat,
> bruised like a forceps baby,
>
> but now he lies
> perfected in my memory,
> down to the red horn
> of his nails,
>
> hung in the scales
> with beauty and atrocity:
> with the Dying Gaul
> too strictly compassed
>
> on his shield,
> with the actual weight
> of each hooded victim,
> slashed and dumped.

In these deeply imaginative poems, we hear Heaney pray that 'some new kind of peace or resolution' will come from all those killed in the violence of modern Ireland, a place and time in which he feels 'lost' and yet 'at home' amid 'the old man-killing parishes'. In Heaney's poems, there is always a sense of the innately generous spirit of men and women. Even when hampered by betrayal, hope persists.

Since a life of poetry, even at its most vital, means living with the persistent fear of silence, the publication of each of Heaney's books seemed a kind of vindication, especially during the later years, when he was writing poems that take the brunt of elegy, ageing, and his own death-work. There was a kind of pendulum swing (his words) away from the outside world of politics back to autobiographical poems, like those he had first published in *The Irish Times*, *The Belfast Telegraph*, *The Kilkenny Magazine*, and *The New Statesman*, though over the decades he wrote many delicately personal lyrics in-between the civic ones. In particular, I think of the sweetly erotic poems of marital love written to his wife, Marie, like 'The Otter', in which he writes: 'I loved your wet head and smashing crawl, / Your fine swimmer's back and shoulders / Surfacing and surfacing again / This year and every year since.'

Throughout the various moments of emphasis in Heaney's poetry – childhood, the deaths of parents, public atrocity, long marriage, ageing – there is a continuous sense of his language being connected to the Irish soil. At his desk, Heaney wrote with a fountain pen that dug like a spade into his own being. Thatching became a metaphor for making poems, divining water was like searching for something in the imagination, and a ploughman turning his plough around at the edge of field (the word for this turning in Latin is *versus*) became a poet turning language into verse. Heaney thought of himself, in the Celtic tradition, as the hermit poet living in a Neolithic hut with an earthen floor and a fire in the hearth. The poet assembling words into art was like a hermit gathering sticks. For Heaney, the word 'poet' still retained an archaic force (unlike the secularized 'novelist' and 'playwright'). Poetry related to chant and song, because it originates from a place in the ear and at the back of the throat, where 'the most common and formed poetics live', he said. The deepest experiences of poetry arrive when some inward reservoir is touched and felt intuitively by the rhythms and meanings that give 'an excitement and passification at once', and as a result awaken 'a space into your whole affect and into your whole emotional nature', he believed.

Reading these two posthumous volumes, selected by Heaney for an edition to be published in Italian translation, I am struck again how fully his poems renew and change my sense of the language of lyric poetry. I am grateful for the violent linguistic substrata that are completely absent in the tepid middle-voice of American poetry today. With rough energy descended from Gerard Manley Hopkins, Patrick Kavanagh, and Ted Hughes – to name only three who opened channels into his language and memory, giving him permission to write poems inspired by his 'guttural muse' – Heaney's poems very quickly naturalize us into their world. Like the tench, a brackish-water fish that feeds on snails and pea-clams on the motionless, muddy river bottom, sending up bubbles, Heaney swims along 'in touch with soft-mouthed life'. In his poems, the guttural vowel is the first place of music. His substrate mud, vowels, and dialect form a completely original nexus unlike anything I know in poetry.

This far-reaching and eloquent selection of poems – mixing guilt with pleasure, mixing quatrains with free verse, mixing sympathy with argument, mixing plain speech with symbolic resonance, mixing Yeats with Dante, mixing pastoral farm life in Derry with underworld violence – reveal a poet gradually becoming simpler and more thoroughly himself, which is the quest of a purist. Heaney's poet's eye was never banished. That 'spacious little fearful part of his being', as he called it, where poetry resides, remained protected. Because of the circumstances of his birth, he grew up in 'a sceptical and exacting milieu', and he approved of this attitude. His work grapples with the actual and the usual. So his poems are not afraid to recognize the demeaning nature of our lives.

But Heaney was a dreamer, too, and we see this in his twelve-lined 'Squarings', where language begins with Prospero-like concreteness and reaches for the hallucinatory spirit of Ariel. The poems in this important mid-life sequence make me think of centaurs, with their sinewy haunches drawn back to the earth and long equine noses, with their human heads, arms, and torsos joined at the horses' withers, where the neck should be. Each of us must work out a relationship between the Prospero and Ariel aesthetics. A handful of 'Squarings' (occasioned, in part, by the death of Heaney's father, a cattleman) are among my favorite Heaney poems.

If the poet is the child of art and life, which are temperamentally opposed, Heaney's poems are always attempting to reconcile the two, just as he was always attempting to reconcile his farm-boy land-sense of poetry with his thoroughly original language sense. Reconciliation was a deep impulse in this beloved poet, who reached for the heights and, attaining them, said poignantly, 'I always feel I have to improve myself.'

Kevin Graham

TRACES

There are things we used to do
like drift under autumn's bright occasion,
how death comes in a thousand colours,
a single crushed reminder.

The air sharpens, tickles where neck
and shoulder meet, loosening a bolt of shivers.
The morning's risen, the mile-long stream
of traffic into town a slow-moving

dream in which drivers contemplate
their lives, unable to lift their heads
in the direction of the park where a colonnade
of oaks breaks sunlight into bars

and flycatchers breakfast on the wing.
The memory of that morning
will come back when, for reasons
better known to yourself, you stepped out

of the car like a movie star, an accuracy
flooding in the margins, a warmth
rising in the blood; all of your futures
suddenly jabbering in unison.

Martina Evans

EVERYTHING INCLUDING THIS ROOM IS A FUTURE RUIN

And when the wind is finished
with us, the rain starts.
I think it will never

stop – worried
by cracks in the wall and
the lump of dislodged lead

that is directing
the rain down into the brick
so that a tobacco coloured

liquid drips down
the inside of the window
and some strange yellow

cauliflowers are growing
inside the kitchen walls.
In 1999 I slept high

in the bird's nest
Marcel and Alice were
kittens and the night after

I took up the fragmenting
1970s carpets, their paws
thundered on the floorboards

frightening me. Now
2014, I've gone to ground
like a badger in the basement

to be close to the garden, my
last great love and the sounds
have changed as the cats jump

from table to floor over
my head and pass in and
out the flap a dozen times.

I hold my heart again.
Donny growls low
in his ginger belly and I see

the fox so close,
his brown-fawn face
like a friend's and it is hard

to see him run from us,
his bare rump –
something's made his fur fall

out and he runs up the spiral
staircase and I run to the backdoor.
I want to welcome him

but he is on the fence and
then Martin's galvanized roof
and gone.

Luke Morgan

CRIB MOBILE

and the whole world
was on it –
that is to say there were people
small and wide-eyed
at the bottom, hanging from drawstring
to buildings, house and sky-scraper
with windows full of cartoon yellow.
Up-string were clouds,
sunny clouds and rainy clouds,
and then birds, planes, balloons –
high-fliers with smiles for
tiny things below.
And at the top, where it drew out
to all of this, was the sun – round
and perfectly bright as a glass light
or the pupil
under a soft closed eyelid.

Paul Batchelor

PRAISE-SONGS

Louise Glück, *Faithful and Virtuous Night* (Carcanet Press, 2014), £9.95.
Peter Fallon, *Strong, My Love* (The Gallery Press, 2014), €11.95.

In 'Education of the Poet', a 1989 lecture later collected as an essay, Louise Glück described her artistic progress as a series of partly-willed, partly-intuitive imaginative leaps: 'Each book I've written has culminated in a conscious diagnostic act, a swearing off'. Sustained over the course of a lifetime, this approach – identifying habits of expression in order to avoid them, setting herself corrective challenges – has enabled Glück to produce a body of work like no other, moving from an identifiably post-confessional stance into a more complex and ambitious understanding of the lyric.

Glück's narrative of self-imposed targets and disavowals may be more useful than the false trails poets often set for readers (one of her abiding themes is how acts of renunciation – refusing to eat, or refusing to speak — can constitute or sustain a sense of self), but it threatens to over-determine the ways in which she is read, and obscure the fact that she never entirely abandons cast-off voices or styles. Her accretive intelligence is clear from the way *Ararat* (1990), with its combination of relaxed, prosy lines and precisely-observed personal detail, has enabled much of her subsequent work. As in *Ararat*, many of the poems in *Faithful and Virtuous Night* strike a conversational tone, but the candid content seems decidedly considered. Oddly, it isn't the candour but the chattiness that sometimes rings false. One newly-acquired stylistic tic is the overuse of qualifications, hedges, and approximations. In one of the longer poems here, 'The White Series', these proliferate to the point of distraction: 'Or, should I say… a kind of… or, to stretch the point… It seemed to me… in the main… as you will guess… Or perhaps… or, more likely… in the main… And yet'. Reading these aloud, they sound like a Beckettian poem – is this where Glück is headed next?

Then again, in light of the book's central question – what do our beliefs count for? – we should expect a degree of uncertainty and provisionality. While there is often a religious cast to Glück's language, it is at the service of declarations of doubt rather than faith, and in 'Afterword' religion itself is defined as 'the cemetery where / questions of faith are answered'. While an earlier poem, 'Celestial Music', concluded with the observation 'The love of form is a love of endings', the title poem to *Faithful and Virtuous Night* opens that statement to question:

> I think here I will leave you. It has come to seem
> there is no perfect ending.
> Indeed, there are infinite endings.
> Or perhaps, once one begins,
> there are only endings.

Another self-imposed challenge is the decision to tell some jokes. I didn't spot the pun in the phrase 'faithful and virtuous night' until it was explained in a poem, which could just be me being obtuse, but I'm hoping that really it's because Glück is the last poet anyone would expect to be a punster. Elsewhere, Glück herself becomes the faithful and virtuous knight, with her heart as the trusty steed: 'Neigh, neigh, said my heart, / or perhaps nay, nay – it was hard to know' ('An Adventure'). There is further humour when she shows self-awareness of her tendency to be portentous (remembering the childhood gift of colouring pencils, she notes 'I soon used up the darker colors'), or else to project her psychological state, as when she listens to the phone ringing:

> I lay in bed, trying to analyze
> the ring. It had
> my mother's persistence and my father's
> pained embarrassment.
>   – 'VISITORS FROM ABROAD'

I assume that, as they do in her earlier work, these figures correspond to Glück's own family: she complicates any confessional tendencies in this book by introducing fictional elements and by establishing the speaker of some of the poems as a male painter, but even the persona poems have roots in her own life and work. 'An Adventure' describes ageing in terms of saying goodbye to the turmoil of love and poetry. Having jettisoned these, Glück seems to have won through into a new silence, but what emerges in that silence is all too familiar:

> faces from the past appeared to me:
> my mother and father, my infant sister; they had not, it seemed,
> finished what they had to say, though now
> I could hear them because my heart was still.
>   – 'AN ADVENTURE'

Perhaps Glück's appetite for formal and stylistic change is driven by a sense that there are some things an artist simply cannot escape – in her case, a Freudian understanding of the family romance.

With its concern over whether and how we can make a good end, *Faithful and Virtuous Night* may not be the best starting place for a newcomer, but Glück is nevertheless a poet everyone should read. It is best to immerse yourself in her work: what seems colourless at first will often reveal itself to have captured a subtle truth; what seems like fussiness turns out to be precision. At her best, Glück challenges the reader to redefine what they understand poetic ambition to be. Her *Collected Poems 1952-2012* repays careful and repeated reading, and will be further enriched by this new volume.

Peter Fallon's *Strong, My Love* brings to mind WH Auden's definition of the poet as one who 'fetches / The images out that hurt and connect'. At several key points in the book, a remembered hurt connects with history, as when the childhood memory of witnessing cattle being dehorned is recalled by a gruesome photograph of the Iraq invasion: 'And Now met Then / when none of us was not bloodstained' ('Law'). The collection's centrepiece, 'Thorn Wire', also begins with a memory of farm labour, as the speaker constructs a thorn-wire fence:

> You've pile-driven the posts
> the sledge would splinter or split.
> You've fastened one end to the strainer
> and unrolled and unravelled
> the other eighty yards of it.

Suddenly, the mundane routine is broken: 'a coiled cobra springs, snags and rips / raw lumps from the back of your bare hand', and then 'I saw blood flow but had no feeling'. Tellingly, Fallon switches from the second person to the first in order to convey a sense of numbed shock. The more predictable move would have been to switch from 'I' to 'you', but the poem is about the intimate sense of coming-to and bewilderment that violence can occasion. Many critics have noted that Kavanagh, Frost and Wendell Berry are significant precursors for Fallon: like theirs his poems are more crafted, and craftier, than they may first appear.

'Thorn Wire' then moves from personal pain to instances of public atrocity, encompassing everything from contemporary crime in the USA to the horrors of two world wars. In its final section, the poem's address opens out even further, without relinquishing any of its focus and authority. We have come a long way from the plain-spoken realism of the opening stanza:

> a whip of guilt
> and greed, of those
> we learned to know
> so well,
> from the open range
> to the cages of Guantánamo,

> all embraced by the devil's rope
> and, now, by mild steel
> galvanize, a chaplet curled
> like a crown of thorns
> around the temple
> of the world.

Like many of these poems, 'Thorn Wire' is cast in what has become one of Fallon's favourite forms: five- or six-line stanzas, with an unobtrusive rhyme on the second/third and the final line. The line-lengths vary, but usually consist of two or three beats, so that, especially when the poem is read aloud, it is often possible to hear something like a hexameter measure quietly asserting itself: having translated Virgil's *Georgics*, as well as (in this collection) poems in elegiac metre by Tibullus, Ovid and Hesiod, Fallon's poetic ear must be ringing with their music.

Although the collection contains many praise-songs to the natural world, and 'A Winter Hymn' sounds a note of hope ('The ghost of winter snows / preserves a promise every February / in snowdrops'), it has an abiding air of solemnity. A note explains that much of the book had been written prior to the deaths of Seamus Heaney and Dennis O'Driscoll, but it feels haunted by loss, or by a more subtle estrangement, nonetheless. Even the declaration of belonging in 'The Fields of Meath' is carefully qualified:

> This is the home place
> now. However far I go,
> should I exclaim,
> I know there'll be the compensations
> of familiar accents in the echo.

Similarly, the title of the collection sounds like an affirmation, but when we encounter it again in the context of 'A Family Tie', we realize that it is an imperative: 'Be strong, my love, / in the broken places'. Still, by asking a loved one to be strong, we give them strength; and Fallon's poems offer a cautious solace, as in the unspoken promise he makes earlier in that same poem: ' "I will mind you in the only state / time is safe, that is, memory" '.

Maurice Harmon

FLIGHT

He was the only one who bolted.

While the rest of us were at our desks
he hurried through an empty hallway,
found his shoes, took his coat, unlocked
the big door, dashed up the cement path.

Small, red-haired, freckle-faced, with thick glasses,
at Hallowe'en recited a poem of such length
I imagined him listening in the cottages, part of something
beyond our school's rigours and routines.

Of course they went after him and brought him back
but I want to record his urgent, sad determination,
his taste for song and story, the seat by the fire
whose heat the rest of us no longer felt.

Liane Strauss

THE GATEKEEPERS

Who guards the gates with the three great locks
        and the crumbling keep
Who trains the vines that entwine the bars
        to protect their sleep

Who shuts the shades, their eyes, the case
        and carves the names
in the granite sky with a marble mind
        Who tends the flames

and puts out the fire Who lies in state
        Who beats time
with an iron pulse while the seep of fate
        Who plays the game

Who appeases doubt, grips a compass faith
        Who shouts the dates
Who reads the signs Who writes the truth
        Who loves the gates

Anne Tannam

FERAL

I remember reading a story once
set in Victorian England
about a gentleman whose young wife
in an unexplained miracle
of the very worst kind
gradually turns into a fox.

And here you are sitting in our kitchen
at a quarter to one in the morning
dressed in someone else's coat
smelling of neglect and nights
without the comfort of sleep.

Are you well?
Such a useless question
when thirst is slowly unravelling summer
from your skin
your hair
your eyes
from the corners
of your mouth.

We offer you the couch
but you are racing across fields
Winter's cold breath pounding in your ears.

Lucy Collins

INDIVIDUAL MEMORIES, SHARED HISTORIES

Eavan Boland, *A Woman Without a Country* (Carcanet Press, 2014), £9.95.
Gerald Dawe, *Mickey Finn's Air* (The Gallery Press, 2014), €10.
Peggy O'Brien, *Trusting Ice* (Orchises Press, 2015), $14.95.

It is difficult to read *A Woman Without a Country* without reflecting on Eavan Boland's long career as one of Ireland's most distinguished poets. Our knowledge of this creative journey profoundly affects how we read this new work – as Boland intends that it should. Since the publication of *Outside History* in 1990 Boland has been primarily concerned with the exclusionary nature of Ireland's historical narratives and their problematic effects on the lives of Irish women; this work has played an important role in shaping the critical discourse surrounding contemporary Irish poetry. Boland's return to key scenes and her reiteration of images – even of phrases – throughout her work remind us how established narratives have a pervasive, even incantatory, cultural power. Yet this repetition takes little account of the fact that the past twenty-five years has been a period of profound change in Ireland, during which our understanding of cultural memory, its operations and effects, has evolved significantly. Boland's repeated return to the landscapes of Ireland in the nineteenth century has kept poverty and exclusion foremost in her readers' minds. Now, in the early twenty-first century, there are many reasons to reflect on such inequalities but it is interesting to note how rarely the pressing realities of contemporary Ireland appear in Boland's work. However, 'Re-reading Oliver Goldsmith's "Deserted Village" in a Changed Ireland' does more than many poems in *A Woman Without a Country* to alert us to the situated nature of the act of reading:

> We were strangers here once. Now
> Someone else
> Is living out their first springtime under these hills.
> Someone else
> Feels the sudden ease that comes when the wind veers
> South and warms rain.
> Would any of it come back to us if we gave it another name?
> (*Sweet Auburn, loveliest village of the Plain*)

The capacity to imagine the lives of others has always been Boland's particular skill, yet syntactical, as well as thematic, familiarity lessens the impact of a number of the poems in this volume. Their accustomed movement between short statements ('I am walking home. A quarter moon rises in the whitebeams') and longer phrases offering a sweeping historical context ('she is // fifty years away from / the worst famine in Europe') sacrifices their evocative power, partly because we encounter not the immediacy of their disclosures but the memory of having read them before in the poet's earlier volumes. The increasingly self-conscious nature of Boland's work is difficult to reconcile with her ethical stance. In this volume she brings the act of reading deliberately to mind and figures the lessons of the past as emerging from books: 'I take down the book. Centuries and years / Fall softly from the page', or 'It happens again / As soon as I take down her book and open it'. This pattern mirrors the intensifying concern with language in her work, her preoccupation with defining words and clarifying exact meanings, as she does when she investigates the etymology of 'cobbler' in 'Nostalgia' or conjures the word 'elver' in 'Cityscape'. Yet in spite of the conclusive opening statement of the latter poem – 'I have a word for it' – these poems show that it is possible for language to render different sensations and memories simultaneously, to trouble the unbreakable bond between the word and the phenomenon it describes. The title sequence interweaves prose passages and poems to a similar end, suggesting the factual context from which the imaginative journey of the poet's forebears can be formed. Yet though Boland's awareness of the relationship between land and sea, between Ireland and elsewhere, is extended here, the strategy of the reclaimed life is less remarkable in this latest volume than it was when it first appeared in her poetry.

Gerald Dawe's *Mickey Finn's Air* is also a book that navigates the past through the material lives of its characters but here the nostalgia – the 'return home' – is sharper and more surprising. This is a short book, comprising just twenty-three poems, but its slightness is belied by the seriousness of its engagement with acts of remembering. The very brevity and precision of the volume challenges the ease with which the past can be deployed in the contemporary lyric, suggesting instead the risk-taking – both creatively and emotionally – that such investigations involve. 'Déjà vu', the book's opening poem, sets the tone: dedicated to the poet's uncle, it interweaves the energies of the man ('the messenger boy, the boy entrant, the spark, the dancer') with the urban spaces he traversed. These identities are expressed in a language at once spontaneous and exact; the power of human connection is celebrated here but the poem is also freighted with losses that are both particular and universal. This layering of personal and cultural pasts is characteristic of the volume as a whole: individual memories are vividly realized yet they evoke shared histories in ways that both explore, and subtly problematize, the basis of community in a fractured country.

Many of the poems move between interior and exterior spaces and, through the materiality of these settings, particular states of mind can be inferred. As well as offering us the between-spaces of city life – the banks and hotels, fairgrounds and football pitches through which friends and strangers circulate – the book explores the thresholds between private and public which permit shared memory to be obliquely questioned. These poems are full of windows and doors, where past and present brush against one another: the broken panes of the old lady's home in 'For Sale', the Velux window traversed by an aeroplane in 'Shortcuts' and, in 'Promises, Promises', the glass walls of empty office blocks – all these suggest the fragility of human attempts at order. Though the book is almost entirely concerned with the past, uncertain futures shadow these poems. Their clarity of expression does not simplify complex experience, however, but confirms the necessity of bearing attentive witness to it. Processes of change are important to the contexts of this volume: in subtle ways *Mickey Finn's Air* testifies to the dramatic alteration that Ireland has undergone in recent decades, but its juxtaposition of the energies of the lived past with the post-crash vistas of 'Every Dog Has His Day' and 'Promises, Promises' suggests that the surfaces of contemporary culture can prompt powerful acts of self-reflection. 'Shortcuts', among the strongest of these poems, connects disparate moments of encounter – fleeting sensory perceptions that might easily pass unnoticed. The contingent nature of all experience is revealed here: the different kinds of light with which the poem begins – 'the light peeled back / from the sky ice-blue'; 'the street lamps shrouded / in mist' – suggest how transient the experience is and just how precise the moment of observation must be. This poem demonstrates how time is layered in this collection: the experience may be rendered with immediacy or through the agency of memory, but is understood uniquely in each case. As the memories become briefer and more intense they are increasingly interwoven with remembered texts:

> the hake, the baked bread, the first cup of tea,
>   the silence in the morning before it all begins,
> the things you miss, the sea in winter,
>   the gorse fires, the field work, the night crossings ...

As this poem suggests, much experience finds its way into language through the act of reading, but the resonance of created art – the first encounter with a poem or song – is one that can only be recalled, never relived.

   By contrast, *Trusting Ice* by Peggy O'Brien seems to place all its hopes in the natural world – in the power of landscapes in which the speaker can be subsumed. This unification of human and more-than-human worlds offers a kind of creative release but it is one that is unevenly registered in this volume. The early poems are directly concerned with snow and ice, drawing attention to changing form and substance in nature as well as in art. Life-giving water becomes hostile, or at least indifferent, to human survival here but the writing process is figured as a way of providing evidence of life in an inhospitable world. 'Tracking in Winter' obliquely likens animal tracks to the formation of the poem – 'Each hoof a cloven nib, / Our testament in snow' – and the speaker's scrutiny of these marks evokes a kind of self-investigation, or textual critique that brings both attentiveness and humility to the process. Other poems, such as 'Night School' and 'New Terrain' enact a similar watchfulness, emphasizing the space of the poem as one of continuous reflection.

The passage of time is important in these works, not so much because they dwell in the past – few of the poems engage explicitly with earlier lives – but because seasonal and diurnal shifts are acutely observed. 'Too Fast' likens the suddenness of nightfall that curtails the child's winter play to the speed with which the individual life passes: 'You're nothing but the track you leave behind, / Parallel lines a jet chalks on the sky'. The simplicity of the final stanza of this poem is far more effective than the busy earlier lines and, elsewhere in the volume too, the tendency to make language do too much obscures both thought and emotion: 'My all too predictable bids to defy gravity, / Helpless sperm word rants, shotgun fluff ('Cat Tails'); 'Please leave a message at the sound / Of the bleeping bleep. I cough, sweat, bleed, blather, hear / Myself blubbering, blush, resolve to be other / Than me' ('Turkey Call'). The sequences, especially 'Tobacco', are somewhat more successful because they offer space for multiple perspectives on a single concept and permit a directness of observation that marks the best of these poems. The speaker's engagement with nature often suggests a kind of rebirth – a way in which the human can become part of that natural world. The complex philosophical questions that this relationship raises are only beginning to be broached in this book.

Annabel Luery

GOLDCREST

As if it isn't miracle enough
that you build your nest with moss
and spider line, that it might breathe
about your growing brood;

or that you dib
into their pinking gapes
the shells of snails and
sometimes single water drops;

you flit between
my collar bones and prise,
from the peedy crannies
of my sleep, cocoons

and springtails, pollen grains;
and so you'll overwinter there –
come spring to tweezer out
the syllables

of your song,
and raise the startling
filaments of your crest, its blaze,
its yellow cadmium.

David Sergeant

THE DOGLEG CORNISH LANES

Stranger, as you may have been, in my dreams again
pleading with me to stay at school (I never missed
    a class) and not to linger
in the dogleg Cornish lanes, each path a rune
    unspoken in the hedgerow's mouth –

this one, taken, leads to a chalice of fields,
its granite cold
    as water in the walker's mouth
and brimming the hills – if you'd drink
    you'd sink

and lie beneath the stream, a belt or brooch
forgotten, orphaned to the speech of clouds
    forgetting everything   throat
now simplified light
    sluice out –

But I always came back. And here I am.

Cherry Smyth

FIRST FLOOR CONVERSION

We were careful, tidy in the new.
And smallness suited it, that small seed
we chose to grow. Our manners were
almost courtly, our behaviour best,
watching for the cling in comfort.

We are rowdy-sturdy now.
And noise needs space to scatter,
rubbing joy, rubbing friction
against a thicker, higher ceiling.
My shoes get under her feet.

Our bed has its own vertical. We climb
and fall and climb its touch infinity,
a grief, like lion to lamb,
a hunger, spaceless,
for the holding home of we.

Ciaran Berry

JUST BODIES

Kei Miller, *The Cartographer Tries to Map a Way to Zion* (Carcanet Press), £9.95.
Deryn Rees-Jones, with images by Charlotte Hodes, *and you, Helen* (Seren Press), £14.99.
Hugo Williams, *I Knew the Bride* (Faber and Faber), £12.99.

Kei Miller's *The Cartographer Tries to Map a Way to Zion* explores how the tongue and the pen chart the boundaries of place and history, often to the detriment of those who live within those boundaries and the particularities of their terrain. Exploring these concerns in his native Jamaica through an extended conversation between two characters, the mapmaker and the rastaman, Miller finds numerous ways to verbally and visually honour a landscape that's complex and fluctuating, that 'does not sit / willingly / as if behind an easel / holding pose' or wait on 'someone / to pencil / its lines' ('What the Mapmaker Ought to Know').

His descriptions of flora and fauna are frequently eye-catching, and there's a tendency towards litany and rhapsody in the presence of natural beauty, as in 'Unsettled' where he describes 'bullet trees so hard / they will one day splinter cutlasses', and 'leh-guh orchids and labrishing / hibiscuses that throw raucous // syllables at crows whose heads are red / as annattos'.

In this extended colloquy, Miller's sympathies rest with the rastaman, who, in the title poem, describes the cartographer's project as one of making 'thin and crushable / all that is big and as real as ourselves'. But he complicates and deepens the conversation too as he explores urges towards a sort of mapmaking innate in 'the haphazard / dance of bees returning / to their hives' and 'the blood / of humming birds' that pulses their 'tiny bodies across / oceans and then back', as well as the rastaman's own looking 'to maps drawn by Jah's large hands'. A sharp sense of wit is brought to bear as well as the poet considers racial and colonial history. The rastaman quips, also in the collection's title poem, that 'Babylon science now confirm – stars too / are "black bodies" ', while the tale of Goldilocks and the Three Bears is rewritten in 'Place Name' as a parable in which the central character 'assumed at once her colonial right to porridge'.

As much as anything else, Miller would draw his readers towards the limits of language, anyone's language, to fully map what he calls, also in 'Place Name', the 'hems and haws / and shrugs of our roads – / how they never run sure, but seem / to arc, bend or narrow, just so'. Thus the problem the collection confronts becomes not solely that of the mapmaker but also of the poet himself or herself, engaged in the struggle between word and thing, aware of the history and weight each word carries.

It's noteworthy too that some of the best poems in this collection occur where the poet steps outside, or slightly to one side, of the conversation that's at the centre of the work. Among the standout poems are 'A Ghazal for the Tethered Goats' that 'do not go to war but send their skins', and two stellar elegies, the intriguingly titled 'A Prayer for the Unflummoxed Beaver' and 'My Mother's Atlas of Dolls'. The latter begins with a mother's request that her more cosmopolitan children bring back dolls from the places they visit, 'as if glass eyes could bear sufficient / witness to where she has not been', a request which leads the speaker to think of how 'we arrange the dead like dolls / set their arms in precise positions', before closing with the candid and deeply moving observation that 'It may have been the dolls that taught // my mother how to die, how to travel / once again, how to say goodbye.'

Deryn Rees-Jones's latest collection also concerns itself with the elegiac and how the living continue in the presence of the dead. A specially commissioned project by the Ledbury Poetry Festival, *and you, Helen* brings out of the shadows the life of Helen Thomas along with, among others, the lives of the poet's grandmother and great grandmother. Helen lost her husband, the poet Edward Thomas, after the battle of Arras in March 1917, a year to the day after he wrote the poem that gives this volume its title. Accompanied by the artwork of Charlotte Hodes, the book is part long poem, part essay.

Rees-Jones's poetry here has a dream-like feel to it, happening often on the edge of sleep or wakefulness, and displaying a compelling sense of time slowed down and free of the clutter of modern life, not to mention electricity and running water. In this space the speaker is able to register the roses that 'blacken in a jug at the bedside', and a hare that quivers 'like an unearthed wire'. The poetry is possessed too of a figurative language that matches its crepuscular quality. Things are always a few steps beyond ordinary: August 'wears ghost selves'; the ash in the grate 'remembers its fire'. It's in this near dream state that the poet gets closer to where 'the dead who are long gone open up their mouths'.

While a conversation with the lost is underway throughout, particularly in the poetry, there's an acknowledgement too, that while the dead are always with us, 'also, and in obvious and important ways, they are not'. Rees-Jones's sense of this fact permeates the entire book. Her own experience as a widow, though only briefly touched upon, is always present, and she explores too the gaps in her knowledge of Helen Thomas and the various relatives she connects Thomas to. 'As always the past rises up to meet us', she asserts, 'riddles its way through our present and future, wobbles, overlaps, runs away'.

In the absence of full knowledge, she imagines humorous scenarios for the lost – Helen falling in with a group of writers in 1920s Paris, Edward seeking a psychoanalytic cure for his melancholia from Carl Jung. The great wisdom of the collection though is what it has to teach us about grief and mourning. The latter demands an engagement 'with the present and the past as well as the future', while the former has the ability to 'permeate and overwrite' all our daily experience, according to the poet. But what is more surprising 'is the intense way in which grief has the capacity to make the sweet sweeter'.

The past, memory, and loss are at the centre, too, of Hugo Williams's *I Knew the Bride*, which takes its title from a Nick Lowe song, here also the title of an impressive elegy for the poet's sister. In a style that's straight talking and self-deprecating, Williams's poems offer a deep, world-weary sense of irony, one that's often most suspicious of his own poetic self. These are the poems of an older man, and there's something refreshingly unadorned about how Williams tackles age. The style is plain, the craft is deft, and there's a strong sense of how the smaller, quieter moments in a life might become large. Like his soul singer, Williams is happy to 'stand still most of the time / and let the words do the talking'. This leads him often to a simple, un-showy wisdom, well illustrated by the six-line poem, 'Falling':

> It isn't so much what
> obstacles we encounter on the way down
>
> as how we come to a stop
> that determines our ultimate condition.
>
> We're OK, as it were,
> so long as we keep falling.

Winningly, Williams has no sense that age has made him any wiser or better, only more resigned to the fact that 'we go on / feeling the same about everything / no matter what happens' ('Love Poem'). These are the poems of someone come, as he suggests in 'A Twitch of the Mouth', to a 'point in the day / when it tips up like a see-saw / and I have to be careful'. Older poets often advise younger poets not to take themselves too seriously; Williams is one of the few who seems capable of taking his own advice.

His humour persists even when his life is at its most challenged. In 'A Recommendation' (part of the long, painful sequence 'From The Dialysis Ward' that ends the book) he quips: 'The beauty of dialysis / is that it saves you the trouble / of planning too far ahead.'

For Williams, humour becomes a means to evade, even momentarily, the betrayals of loss and illness. This is something we see in his honing in on the 'white Stetson / from a Country music catalogue' that rides atop his deceased sister's coffin as it disappears into the crematorium flames in the title poem. It's there as well in 'Ray's Way', his portrait of a fellow patient who enters the ward shouting 'MY NAME IS BOND' before emptying his bag of 'beer cans, biscuits', and 'betting slips'.

There are points though where the humour is less successful. It's hard to laugh with the old rogue in 'Acteon', 'torn apart' by the 'little pointed teeth' of all his ex-girlfriends, and harder still to not be put off by the sexual politics of 'Twenty Yards Behind' ('If we knew their true response, / as they threw their limbs around / to all the things we find so intense // we might experience detumescence'). The guise of the older male as a kind of bumbling Martian figure always out-thought and out-fought by his female counterpart fails here. It feels dated and predictable, and the fact that it's a note played perhaps in full knowledge of who or what it might upset doesn't make it any more appealing.

It's a pity, because elsewhere Williams's take on life after love, as with his consideration of illness and loss, is arresting and insightful. In 'Bar Italia', from the sequence 'Now That I've Forgotten Brighton', the poet looks through the window of the establishment where he and a former love used to meet, and experiences, through memory, an out-of-bodiness in which the couple are 'so near I can almost touch us'.

This out-of-bodiness crops up too in 'New Year Poem', where the poet describes how 'My eyes look over my shoulder, / avoiding my gaze', and in 'Eucalyptus' where he writes 'I rise to my toes at the top of the stairs / and my body passes before my eyes'. Perhaps Williams's best gift to us is this frankly reported sense of how, more and more with age, mind and body begin to separate, how the weight of memory gradually drags us away from our physical selves.

David Wheatley

from 'MAKING STRANGE'

Ce navire est à nous et mon enfance n'a sa fin.

I remember – no, not remember what does not end.

Already the warm dark is taking its leave of me.

I'm not going back.

Isn't he the image of her, the living image?

Borne from the city down one of two routes that divide at the Dodder and the Irish Sweepstake Building, the lottery of the high or the low road yielding the same small jackpot, home.

A cuddly toy on a grabber in Dawson's Amusements: hooked, hoisted and (wait for it) dropped.

There are other cuddly toys; there is no other town. Shudder go the floorboards as the ghost train rattles round its circuit, and again as the black and amber diesel dawdles past to Wexford, train upon train but only one destination for you – can we always live in Bray, Mam? – the pincer of Bray Head and the harbour's fingers holding the prize in place, never to be let go.

A cup of mashed-up bread and water, then someone closing his eyes and sticking his finger in it: Nelson's eye. The invisible past a glutinous pulp between your fingers, a long-dry socket suddenly moist again.

Across the sea came Mantán, the gap-toothed, crazed in the head, chanting impiety, jeered at and stoned.

Wicklow a slack-jawed skull on the map, chewing on Carlow, sideburned with hills, and the back of its head full of swans in the harbour and me.

Flick of the Town Hall wyvern's tail.

The babe-in-arms shrieks and demands to be lowered to play on the hexagon tiles on the hotel floor. All touches, connects, bites and locks together.

Do not touch me: I do not wish to be touched ('when you finish combing my hair I will have finished hating you').

Did you ever in your life hear the like of it!, says Mam.

Held upside down while my hair is shampooed and rinsed in the kitchen sink, then righted again, and attempting to suckle the taps' two witchy-blue spouts.

Pee-puddle spreading speculatively over the PE hall floor where I sit. Then dragged off to the boys' room by Auntie Brenda, soggily disgraced and unrepentant.

Sure you have my heart scalded!

Sinbad the ragdoll sailor, our narrator, voyages nightly below the pillow, surfs the hot water bottle's gurgling currents before resurfacing, breathless. Pyjama atolls lurk there, treacherous Dinky car reefs.

Darting from the car to the door you – I blurring into you – you beat on the glass and smash it. In case of emergency break glass. Knocking on glass today it is the scars of that other pane you feel on the ridge of your palm.

The door opens onto the dust of years and a space of light and empty waste (memory, that lumber room) – no, wait, onto rashers for tea and the telly on in the next room. Not rashers again!

Under and inside the table it is Moonbase Alpha, above and outside it is the 1940s, land of obligatory beetroot. Eat it all up now. Grandad is eating cabbage and fatty bacon in his waistcoat. That biro will have your eye out and no mistake.

Have you been over beyond to Derrylossary, he asks his brother. Would y'ever see about them slates from Calary. I have. I will. The whole shebang. The barometer needle has never been observed to move. You set it to Fair and the weather immediately improves.

Under the table is Moonbase Alpha but overhead is Skylab, doomed and seeking only your head in the crowd before it chooses its moment and – no, not yet. Your packet of Space Dust catches the meteor shower in its wake, bubbles popping all along your tongue where they crashland.

Twitch-buzz of a dying fly on the sitting room windowsill. An odour of death leaks from the Vapona hung from the ceiling, mixed with the Mr Sheen sharp in the airless room where Mammy is cleaning. Scour, wipe and spray, hide in your room while she.

Have you been at the chocolate again?, the airtight bag of it hoarded under the bed for Lent. Out with that Toblerone this minute!, the semi-chewed triangle spat into the kitchen sink to bob in the soapy dishwater.

The grasshopper tickles a song from its belly.

47! And this one? 53! And this one?, your school nurse questioner flipping the binder pages, its numbers hidden like camouflaged shells on the beach. Not colourblind then. And now for a quick root around in – *ahem* – that's a good lad – cough when I say.

Peanut butter and buttercup brown and yellow of the rusting chairlift on Bray Head. Next stop the cross, says Mammy, pretending. Make Daddy carry you anyway. Carry, carry me, Daddy!

Three inferior copies of me, reproducing all my virtues and none of my flaws. Whose legs are they in the bed? Kicky Malicky. Number one has a little hair at the base of his thumb, just so, like mine, has always had. Asked about this years from now he will flatly deny it. Perhaps number two, number three, perhaps no one.

Reach for a nail-clippers and yank the hair out. The words 'Philip is cool' in spidery biro in the bottom drawer of a wardrobe, rediscovered during a house move in England thirty years later and left there.

Hollow leathery thwack off the wall in Canon Crinion's handball alley. Old repeater, echo-chamber: strike it again.

There was the Triumph estate with the Mickey Mouse transfer on the bonnet that always made you carsick until we hung those strips from the bumper. Then there was the Alfa Romeo. Your brothers loved the Alfa. That would have been when your father had that beard of his hanging off his chin. Then there was the Mirafiori with a growl on it like you wouldn't believe from the clutch. Tell me, how does that old jalopy of yours keep going at all?

That's the way! A weakness for railway stations among the harmless mad. A worn old briefcase in one hand full of, what is it, pebbles or sand, he waves the Rosslare train on its way. Easy now: and she's off!

CIÉ would like to apologize for the late arrival of the Connolly Train on platform one. This train is approximately forty years late.

The osprey feather in her trilby has fallen to earth from a genteeler pre-war decade. Ms Tyner of Ashford produces Aunt Maud's photograph album, smoothing it open on her rooftop snaps of 1916. In this one here you can see, to one side of the rubble, the elephant over Elvery's door, the sporting outfitter's. Of course they thought she was a sniper and took pot-shots back at her, which she didn't like one little bit. And what did we do then, Mam? Were we alive then?

On his longest and most treacherous journey Sinbad will set out on a wee-wee tide beyond the known world of the bed sheets, where he will be captured and hung out to dry in Cuxhaven, Germany, home of grandfatherly walruses. Poor drowned Sinbad spoken of henceforth in whispers, needing only a tide of fellow seamen to wash him back home, but too soon for that, then re-emerged from under a pile of socks in Dad's suitcase. As he was saying earlier –

Run to the phone and ring when the mystery voice comes on the radio. Nanny says wireless. Engaged. Long wait for the 9 to rotate back when you ring. In the call box you press button A, or B, I forget. Which one was A and which one was – , I might ask now, on the phone to – I'll just hand you over to your… – , If I can just get a word in – , Which one was what, button what?, Did you know we have free calls now so I can … –, As I was SAYING – , Oh, forget it!

The papal contrails peter out fluffily over the playground, the rapier-tips of Master Lavin's index fingers jabbing Hail Marys skyward: what's that doing on *Newsround*? See what's on the other side. Cartoons, I hope. Young people of Ireland I …, something something, the LP Granny buys of his visit scratched to unplayable and repeating: Young people of, young people of …

From the burrawang tree falls Grug, one more teatime cartoon, his caveman hair a shock of fronds and vines. No, don't remember that one. You don't expect me to know them *all*, do you?

The middle room in Nanny's we never sit in has a panel in the wall, awaiting a sudden peekaboo! through to the sitting room, to teacups and custard creams dropped in surprise. Isn't he the card. Bright as a button too! I'll say. Then off to see what Seánie is burning in his back garden today, black bituminous plumes twisting down the road all the way to The Punnet.

Salubrious waft of Mr Lynch the piano tuner's pipe smoke and a jabbing thumb on an upright Bechstein's middle C. Abrupt report of a tuning fork smacked on the sideboard, then stood to vibrate at concert pitch C. *Ker-thwonk*! Strike that note again. Something wrong there, says Sinbad. That's some dose, says Mam. Then when it's fixed, All tickety boo, says Dad. Open the piano lid when Mr Lynch departs and make fairy music, plucked harmonics, on the strings, then close the coffin lid over them, sealing them in, in the dark.

Well in the merry month of May, sings Dad in the Tara Towers Hotel when in comes a billy-goat man, all primary colours like the test card – Luke Kelly – knocks back a – what's that called Dad, that's not a pint – gin and tonic and leaves – Hoor's drink!, shouting as he goes – is that a rude word?

Servants of St Bridget, the oystercatchers lined up on Booterstown Strand. A Bridget's cross on the RTÉ test card, not the girl with the clown and the blackboard. Noughts and crosses it is then. No wait, I *meant* to put the x in the middle: start again. Look Mam, Oxo, just like the cube! Then Rubik's cube. One side done. Peel off the stickers, all primary colours and cheat. Look, Mam, look!

If the crab on the beach could only try to walk sideways, he would go straight.

The train trip from Bray to Greystones a series of empty stages – tunnel, cove, tunnel, cove – between the tracks and the sea, or framing a ferry, a freighter, rows of cormorants unmoved in the stalls, where the signal shelter sits windowless but occupied, *casa dei doganieri*, its line of chimney smoke pulled out to sea where the fulmars' foul mouths scream and spit.

The Harbour Bar to the Brandy Hole, my life by water –

Cuprous old penny placed on the tracks as the diesel passes, recovered afterwards slightly flattened but none the worse for that. Then pocketed for the penny falls in the Star Amusements, the leaping salmon on my last ten-pence piece saved for the Space Invaders. The train door snaps back, the penny drops, and well before teatime invaders have conquered the earth.

Its green patina scraped off the old penny, dog shit picked from my
runners with a stick in the garden (*have you checked the other one too?*).
Cover a sheet in crayons for Master Cronin, cover the colours in
black then remove with the back of a spoon to reveal unsuspected
stick-men below, lurking henceforth in every darkness, fiery-orange
and red homunculi dancing in the fire after tea.

Tá daidí ag obair, tá mamaí sa chistin. But Mammy is working and
Daddy is in the kitchen, chopping the mince, conjugating gender
roles and irregular verbs. The rude words not in the dictionary. Action Man is smooth down there, when you check. Dolls you can't
speak for. Cough now, the nurse says again, the cheek of it: I have
balls! I have two balls!

He does be liking his tea at five, amn't I after telling you. Frequentatives of corned beef and mash, dialectal isobars visible on the weather
forecast map at the end of the news. But first – plate balanced on
your knees while you eat – time for *Ivor the Engine*.

C – E – G – C– G –E – C. G – B – D – G – D – B – G. D – F – something wrong there. Sharp, sharp! Half-hour's practice before school
in the morning, the neighbours loving it, *2000 AD* up on the stand
while you do the arpeggios then falling into your lap.

Then during the war Bridie went to London, says Dad back from a
funeral – went to London, said the priest, and met Dan Dare. Can
you imagine it, Dan Dare. The Mekon leans forward on his flying
dish (puny spaceman, what can you do against my unlimited power)
before dismissing the earthling and levitating off about his business,
the extermination of all human life, then a bike-ride down the
stream with David and David and Alan and Maurice and Dáire.

Uncle Ted, wheezing elephant seal of a man dressed in burgundy
and mustard, pulls up in his Wolseley, walnut-effect dash and radiator badge fresh from a Sunday waxing. In driving gloves, too. He
bears a Christmas offering of mouldy biscuits, nibbled, discarded.
Glass of sherry? Only the one, thanks, the smell of damp corduroy
warming in front of the fire, sickly, old-mannish. Or maybe another,
he reconsiders, while I'm here.

Eyes level with the counter of his featureless shop, Mr Delimata
stares through the window at his trim Wartburg outside, facets of
distant Polish beginnings visible through his jeweller's eyepiece. The
old country, the new country. The other country. Uncle J dead in

Zürich, cousin L over in England. On his wife's side, this would be. What's for Christmas dinner? Then a Chopin mazurka or two on the piano and a walk round the harbour, knots of the overfed bored still wearing the hats from their crackers and offering Christmas cake to the swans.

First Confirmion, I mean Confirmunion, a badly knotted tie and odours of chrism and incense; body of something stuck in the roof of your mouth. More Space Dust handy for that. Still, worth a digital watch. A clutch of balloons escapes at the end and bump against the church ceiling like the levitating Joseph of Cupertino, making a holy show of himself at mass again. You work the wafer free and it bobs straight back up whence it came.

Your front teeth complete a slow approach, touch and cross. The crumbs of decades will collect there, collect there still. Drunken molars buckling this way and that, tiny Judases wanting their thirty pieces of silver. Fabled crustacean, your brace lurks in its glass of water at night, with a nasty bite on it for the unwary: ouch!

That was our house where those officers were shot in their beds, Ms Tyner continues. My father was sure that but for the door he put in at the side, the shootings would never have happened, and felt very guilty. I remember meeting Michael Collins, Mr Ó Broin tells Dad, he gave me a watch. Pressed it very firmly into my hand. An upright coffin of a grandfather clock strikes and an antique kettle comes to the boil in the kitchen. Then later a mechanical coffee pot drives onto the pitch in Croke Park, Bray, and opens fire on the crowd, Neil Jordan directing. Black and Tans out, Brits out of the Prince of Wales Terrace, the Carlisle Grounds now! – *And, cut!*

Finish your beetroot, there's a good man, eat it all up! Granny's cheeks the same ruddied purple by now, you flinching from the vitamin flush and the kiss goodbye afterwards.

Over the high wall by the house goes a schoolbag slung and a trespasser-dawdler fearing the slavering dogs only for hastening him on his way. Over the wall goes a football now spiked in gehennas of brambles, offside anyway, a low *pfft* of relief escaping its bladder. When objects collide or explode in space they do so in silence.

Skylab falls.

Ireland comes unstuck and moves to the centre of the map, Christian Brothers following the arrows and scattering round the globe, Ireland the navel, umbilically linked to the little black babies. One fruity stray trouser salute during singing and Brother Horgan cancels our trip to the mushroom farm.

Master Barry's quick hand traces, conceals a digit on the blackboard. What was it? Quicker than the wrong answer the chalk propelled through the air, its contact with you smarting still.

A seagull takes aim and deposits its load of guano smack on Brother Forde's dome in the playground one morning: remembered or imagined, imagined-remembered?

Stay there till we put out the rubbish, I said. Brother Justin again. Yet when you emerge it is Brother Justin and all his kind who have departed.

The *Record Breakers* man plays albums by feeling the grooves and singing the tunes. Get thumbprints all over yours and – no, doesn't work. Then try them backwards and devil this, devil that, you've been led to believe – no, doesn't work either. Try 'Rockin All Over the World': drag the needle backwards and – can't hear anything – the needle jumping out of your hand like a boom down the harbour. And I like it, I like it, I – must be scratched – gets a bit boring. The needle bored too, falling asleep on its pillow of fluff at the end, firing off rhythmical snores like Trigger the dog, I mean Mitch.

Unpeel their sellotape and release the plastic Spitfires stuck to the cover of *Warlord* and *Victor*, owl-pellets of someone else's war: their line grounded decades later in the lifesize model outside an abandoned Airfix factory in Hull, East Yorkshire, opposite the smelting furnace, graffitoed *I love you Mam*.

Blind amoebas swim in the tray in Mr Owens' dark room, from your go on the antique box camera one Sunday. Low tide's fugitive meniscus outside the Harbour Bar washing over the simple box camera lens: snap. Sheepskin coat, woolly hat, and the tail-end of Mam's Jackie Onassis hair-do – Jackie who? – snap. A sticker marked 'free' on the spoils: some puddle of black and white mess, events that occurred less than once hereby memorialized.

Jared Harel

MASTERS OF THE UNIVERSE

I need to clock someone, split skin,
but the evening is being so god-
damn agreeable, the city
like a sibling fixing my flat,
so instead I buy socks, jeans tight
enough to chafe my thighs.
Wasn't I the kid with no preference
in colour, fine with whichever
slice was mine? While others
crushed insects and busted lips,
my battles featured plastic
action-figures – break a limb
and they still wouldn't blink.
I didn't think I needed vengeance,
not when Ben Dobrowski
stole my He-Man, or Peter Barkoff
called me fag. But now, it's as if
I never knew me. I might
as well be Samson, hair wild,
captive in a castle aching to snap.

Alan Gillis

NOTHING ESCAPES HIM; HE ESCAPES US ALL

Stephen Enniss, *After the Titanic: A Life of Derek Mahon* (Gill and Macmillan, 2014), €29.99.

Derek Mahon's poem 'Ode to Björk' begins:

> Dark bird of ice, dark swan
>   of snow, your eyes bright gamine
> teardrop Inuit eyes
>   peep from a magazine
>
> as if to say 'Fuck off
>   and get my new release;
> you don't know *me*, I am
>   the dark swan of ice
>
> and secrecy ...'

Envisaging Björk with a megaphone, telling the world 'like Garbo / "I want to be alone!"', Mahon imagines she wants, instead, 'mystery and mystique', and yearns for 'the hidden places where / the wild things are and no one / can track you to your lair'.

Stephen Enniss ends this attempt to track Mahon to his lair with an Afterword, explaining how Mahon, after initial cooperation, withdrew his support and became increasingly anxious about its publication. Enniss might have foreseen as much. From the beginning, Mahon's verse has abounded with scepticism and fascination regarding our thirst to know another truly, questioning whether such knowledge is possible, or indeed desirable. 'The Life We Know' begins: 'I will not be known by what I did or said'. One of his key poems, 'Lives', expands the limits of a single life in a manner that is effortlessly virtuosic and entirely unsettling, as so much of Mahon's verse is. The result is deeply head-bending, and ends with a warning:

> I know too much
> To be anything any more;
> And if in the distant
>
> Future someone
> Thinks he has once been me
> As I am today,

>   Let him revise
>   His insolent ontology
>   Or teach himself to pray.

The poem is, of course, about more than mere biography, but its dazzling sabotage of the idea that we might inhabit the essence of a person, or thing, or zeitgeist, and indeed its warning against the arrogance of such temerity, is not something that should be discounted as the pose of one particular poem. For Mahon, the will to put someone in their place, to account for them, to 'know them', unveils a will to power that is upsettingly banal and simplifying. It is of a piece with the imperialistic accountancy of the information age, with the commodification and control of our interior world. In 'Harbour Lights', he writes: 'The new dark ages have been fiercely lit / to banish shadow and the difficult spirit'.

Nonetheless, Enniss has taken considerable pains to shine a light on this difficult spirit. For years, he was the overseer of Emory University's archives, which holds the largest collection of Mahon's papers (and those of many of his peers). As one might expect, the book's strength lies in its use of Mahon's letters. From these, we get a keen sense of a complex and witty man, intelligent and sensitive yet impish and urgent, often embattled yet resourceful within the maelstrom of his life's ups and downs. Mahon emerges as an enthralling, maddening paradox of self-insight and self-blindness. We also get fascinating forays into discarded poems and drafts of published poems, especially from the early years. Mahon's has been a life of many travels and differing abodes, a constant stream of criss-crossing exits and returns, and this book serves a great function in mapping his transits. Mahon emerges from his *New Collected Poems* as a poet of Belfast, of Dublin, of London, of New York, of Kinsale, and of further climes, and it's a boon to his readers to have the charts of this odyssey. And given the bumpy ride Mahon has given readers, regarding the chronology of his poems, this biography is also welcome in giving a clearer context concerning the writing of individual pieces (it's more difficult to discern in which year what poem was published, with Mahon, than perhaps with any other contemporary poet of comparable status, given the several remixes of sequencing these poems have undergone). Indeed, Enniss provides an invaluable list of Mahon's poems by date of first publication as an appendix. For all these reasons, the book is worth the price of admission, and will provide an enabling source of reference for Mahon's readers.

Yet there are problems. While it is good to have a sense of when and where poems were written, Enniss tends to make them passive reflectors of life's circumstance. Mahon's poems primarily serve to colour Enniss's chronicle. And while this may be the biographer's prerogative, it's insufficient when the poems are clearly so much more than incidental. My understanding is that Mahon believed that Enniss was embarking upon a critical study of the poems, then withdrew his cooperation when he saw it was mere biography, its emphasis hugely on the man and not the work. Enniss explains that Mahon subsequently tried to censure the coverage of differing events and personages, and so the parting of ways became inevitable. But more than this, the implication is that Mahon's withdrawal was of a psychological piece with the emotional insecurity Enniss finds throughout the life – another crisis, typical of a life full of crises – because this tale of Mahon narrates a ceaseless trail of wreckage, of family, friends and colleagues let down, commitments reneged on, opportunities lost or spurned. Enniss explains that Mahon himself tried to write a memoir, but abandoned the project as there was so much to be ashamed of.

For Enniss, Mahon is a poet of suffering. And behind his catalogue of crises lies a cultural-historical perspective, an overriding narrative of Mahon's troubles in accounting for his background, and for the Troubles, which disables him from finding his proper place in the scheme of things. Whether or not Enniss is correct in this, one would concede that his job was to relate a life that has contained a deal of instability and contradiction. Enniss tells of how a 'reporter for a local newspaper' attended a seminar taught by Mahon at Wake Forest, then published an article about it, concluding that 'Mahon is perhaps not the most consistent of individuals'. Indeed Mahon, in these pages, becomes synonymous with unreliability, and we get much evidence that he might have been the most feckless teacher in the western world. Yet Mahon clearly thought so himself, and evidently he didn't want to teach, but was cornered into it for financial reasons. And one wonders if some form of sympathy might not have been possible. In this small example, what could be more awful than having a reporter in the room, analyzing you, when trying to teach a poetry seminar? What kind of creature could be comfortable?

Enniss would have known before starting that Mahon suffered from years of alcoholism. Perhaps he felt that a 'warts and all' element to his narrative was unavoidable. Yet no real compassion emerges in terms of understanding a man with a chronic illness. He would have also known beforehand that Mahon's marriage broke down. There were other women in his life. And one wonders at the overriding tone of censure. It's not that a biographer should expunge their subjects of responsibility for faults (Mahon himself seems scorched, almost paralysed with self-remorse at times). But with an absence of empathy, this book becomes rather tabloid. We get the picture quickly, after which the remorseless piling on of facts becomes unenlightening. The point of this life-writing seems to be to suggest Mahon should have pulled his socks up, should have been more consistent, and so on. But a steady job, efficient professionalism, a successful marriage, and so forth, provide no real watermark for poetic endeavour.

The real problem resides with the underdeveloped sense of Mahon's poetry throughout Enniss's book. Without adequate engagement with this, the life is bound to seem a shell. Enniss relates that Mahon indicated he felt his recent, summary publications with The Gallery Press – *New Collected Poems, Echo's Grove, Selected Prose, Theatre* – constituted an autobiography of sorts. Taking the former alone, one indeed reads the magisterial sweep and depth of that extensive tome as a spellbinding account of a many-sided, intricate, profusely rich sensibility; a book of vulnerability and defiance, endlessly probing and susceptible. The point, surely, is that it transcends any sense of a single life to become a book of our sensibility, our experience, through the multitudinous validation it offers by enlarging our own lives through imaginative capacity. Without a sense of this imaginative dimension, Enniss's life flat-lines.

Mahon's distaste for his own biography may well stem from a wish not to have his dirty linen held up in public. But his scepticism more deeply stems from a core interest of his art, which asks us to consider most fully: *What is a life?* From there, his work queries: *What is culture? What is history? What is reality?* It is an engine of profound philosophical inquisitiveness. And Mahon's restlessness, on these questions, is one of his chief artistic weapons. Enniss views the life as some form of failure, but makes the drastic error of allowing the poems to become mere images of this interpretation. For Enniss, it seems, all the flaws that he narrates flow from an inadequate response to the primal scene of Mahon's origins. This leaves Mahon seething with guilt, mortally aggravated by a wounded sense of personalized complicity with the historical wrong of the Northern Irish state's apartheid, scattered to the winds by the horror of the Troubles.

In one sense, there can be no doubt that Mahon's sensibility emerges out of the suffocation of identity politics. There is no evidence to suggest Mahon has ever thought that one isn't conditioned by where one is from, perhaps fundamentally so, and he certainly never shirked this; but throughout his career he has had to battle against overweening reductionism. The other side of the coin, his work insists, is all the other things that one might be, not readily identifiable through the accident of origin. Such tensions between necessity and freedom provide the grounds of much of his work, which is to say that ambivalence is paramount to his work: 'By / Necessity, if not choice, I live here too.'

Mahon's origins delivered him to the world as a Protestant from the North of Ireland, working-class and urban. A working-class Protestant background, in this context, means hard-core Calvinist, with overtones of severity and brutalism, different in kind to the relative liberalism of Anglican middle-class Protestantism. Essentially, for Enniss, Mahon is from a realm that is inherently anti-poetic. It might be expected that he'd be troubled by these origins, but whether Enniss is right to foreground the crux as a central crisis in the life and career is another matter. In this narrative, Mahon's education at a posh school, and then Trinity College, takes him on an upward trajectory, from whence he is plunged back into a severe identity crisis when the outbreak of the Troubles reveals he has not properly explored, reflected upon, and assimilated his recalcitrant cultural beginnings. But the problem is that Enniss seems discontented by Mahon's response. To be sure, one can see an alternate recoil, in Mahon's verse, between facing up to, and rejecting, the circumscriptions of his background. Indeed, Mahon wouldn't be worth the bother if guilt and vexed angst weren't in the mix. They are, with potent force. But Enniss implicitly longs for a resolution, for a formal, harmonising and enduring mythos. In this, Mahon seemingly lets him down.

The given of history and origins, throughout Mahon's work, are never treated with anything less than a double-edge. 'One part of my mind must know to learn its place.' This famous line, from what is now the first poem in Mahon's *New Collected*, seems to cement Enniss's narrative. Only the line is, of course, dripping with irony. To tell somebody to learn their place is synonymous with saying 'don't get above yourself'. And Mahon was partially saying 'screw that!' Other parts of his mind, one could infer, might learn other things. The 'Last of the Fire Kings' underlines this aspect of the sentiment. Its speaker wishes to escape, but 'the fire-loving / People, rightly perhaps, / Will not countenance this', and demand that he 'inhabit, / Like them, a world of / Sirens, bin-lids / And bricked-up windows', insisting that he 'die their creature and be thankful'. This poem is about engagement with history rather than learning one's place. But the difference is negligible: we are still talking about a negative, an awful reduction. The people are probably right, and the idea of freedom is possibly a chimera. But nonetheless, Mahon's tone of reluctance and contempt, his churlish (and indeed withheld) acceptance of responsibility, strikes most forcibly. And this ambiguity provides the poetic voltage. Even the self-recrimination of 'Afterlives' is ambivalent:

> Perhaps if I'd stayed behind
> And lived it bomb by bomb
> I might have grown up at last
> And learnt what is meant by home.

'Perhaps' speaks volumes. Perhaps he wouldn't have learned a thing. That Mahon perhaps learned more by taking the nomadic, unsettled, uprooted and stressful course that he did, in his life, is not something Enniss is willing to countenance.

The unspoken but central structuring principle of this book is that Derek Mahon is not Seamus Heaney. Catholic, rural, harmonising and optimistic, seemingly embodying a redemptive central narrative built upon identity and belonging, allegorical of a broader historical righting of an intrinsic political wrong, and every inch a successful 'smiling public man': almost all the facets of the Heaney story are warped and frustrated in this story of Mahon. Without, for one second, wishing to belittle the achievement of Heaney (Irish poetry criticism is plagued by the fallacy that talking one thing up means talking another thing down), the problem with making Heaney central to one's sense of contemporary Irish poetry, even if implicitly, is that this doesn't acknowledge the anomalous nature of Heaney's career. Not everyone is like Seamus, and while Heaney's career as a whole offers an image that becomes a touchstone to us, it is not the only one.

In short, when Mahon suggests that getting away might be as poetically apt as going home, when he puts radical ambivalence about background and community to the fore, when his career evidences unevenness regarding the social obligations of poetry, when the interrelationships between Irishness and globalized internationalism are pervasive, and no clear line is drawn between them, and when these destabilizations are made the central ground of the work: there seems every reason to say that Mahon is a paradigmatic Irish poet of our time. When he seems to simultaneously reject and explore the circumscriptions of his background with searing ambivalence, the results are poetically inspired, translatable to readers from all kinds of backgrounds. Enniss frequently has Mahon searching for an Irish historical narrative that might serve as a valid 'objective correlative' for his poetry. That he never really finds one sums up, for Enniss, his shortcomings. But was he looking for one? Enniss doesn't stop to ask whether such a conceit would really be credible; he never asks, in a positive light, what poetry might gain if it insists that all history is fragmented, barbaric, and insidious. In a letter to Jimmy Simmons, Mahon stated: 'the liberal position is untenable in the face of human nature, the evidence of history'. He quickly added: 'I grant you no other position is tenable either, or not for long'.

As it happens, this in turn somewhat misrepresents Mahon, whose cultural sense of Ireland was made readily apparent in his co-editorship, with Peter Fallon, of *The Penguin Book of Contemporary Irish Poetry* in 1990. It's an open-minded and open-eared vision of non-programmatic, representative inclusivity. He's a united Ireland man, utterly disinterested in the exclusivity of the North. Why did Enniss not make more of this? One surmises that it's because Mahon has rigorously avoided making a noise about it, has scrupulously side-stepped any sense of it being 'a position', as if to stave off any pats on the back. Any such grandstanding, one can see, would quickly become intolerably reified and static for him. Put Mahon in his place, and he'll quickly slip out the back door, suitcase in hand. But the apparent casualness disguises a consistent and searching commitment, and the contingency that results – the sense that there are bigger things to worry about, other terrains to consider – somewhat complicates the critic's drive for familiar frameworks, dismantles the usual paradigms.

In Enniss's book, the discombobulating range and overt mask-wearing of Mahon's verse, along with his unyielding ambiguities, ultimately come across as a weakness, which seems absurd. His insistence that Mahon is a laureate of suffering accounts for many aspects of the work, but it disregards the oeuvre's powerful uplifts, deep humanitarianism and hard-won but authentic affirmations. Not to mention its brilliant wit. Meanwhile, the sense of failure Enniss finds in the life begins to problematically confuse subject matter and artwork. The failure of culture, of the self, of economics; the sense of epistemological breakdown, of ecological disgrace: what else should be the central subjects of our poetry? The unsettled edge of his poems about home and historical responsibility, the mixing of musical sensuality with piercing rational scepticism, along with the imaginative enlargement of engaging with many places and multiple sensibilities: these are things that make Mahon indispensable, make his work a necessity, a triumph of ambition and achievement.

One final problem with the book is that its level of detail completely falls away after the publication of *The Yellow Book* in 1997. The great poetic harvest of what follows from Mahon, in the twenty-first century, is basically untouched. Neither does the book engage with the nature of his poetic gear-shift, from coiled dramatic lyric to a more expansive and reflective style. Many readers, of course, still cling to the earlier work first and foremost. But especially when reading *New Collected Poems* front-to-back, the importance and value of the work from the last twenty-five years becomes crystal clear. Recent poems such as 'Monochrome' and 'Dreams of a Summer Night' provide the most eloquent and necessary coda to this biography. Mahon, it turns out, may well be one of our great poets of healing also. There is a great deal of his art that is yet to be assimilated by readers. The corpus is there for generations to come. Enniss's book is a useful, flawed, problematic report on aspects of a troubled career, but the poetry is elsewhere.

Kathleen O'Brien

WILD IRIS

That old mother humming
on the strand,
she plants flowers
in the sea's mouth.

She thinks her father drowns
among the reeds
and finds a wild iris
to put on his grave.

In the moon's blue house
she sings
for her shadow children,
their paths washed clean.

Macdara Woods

IN TOMIS HE REMEMBERS

Is this how we end
In distance
You are all too beautiful
I am too old

Long cactus years
And roads
And brutal corrupt politics
Have intervened

Time is distance here
True distance not
Spiny silence between
Place and place

And where you are
Such closeness
As still gnaws at me in age
Untouchable

And longing to be touched
Again
Just one time more
Before it ends

Too old for that rich
Milk of almonds
Too late for phantom cab rides
With your lovers

Tomas Unger

HAY

At last at rest against bales, there I am, lying in the back cart
of a farmyard truck or car, staring out as nothing but endless
field falls away before us. I can't even hear my siblings
beside me, so know they're there, all of us listening as
the engine mows silence, yes, but it grows back as grass.

I've lived for eight or so years. Just minutes ago I was
picking more apples than I could ever hold, as though
to go and hide and hoard them where no season could change me.
This must be the story of lives I've lived. Once I was
a mad gatherer. Then, sheer starer, a stare. Hay somewhere after.

Desmond Graham

THE CHANGELING

lifting out the photograph
she points to the small girl
with long legs and a surprised look
at ten – her daughter

this is the person she knows still
and talks about
and hears sometimes
answering in her head

it is not that her daughter
as she now seems to be
is not quite wanted
just that how much better it would be

if she could only learn
that when her mother talks of her
she means this pigtailed girl
and not the woman she is now

and when her daughter says
'Look – there's me in the photograph
I can't believe it – can you –
I was just ten then'

her mother smiles
at the young girl in the picture
wondering that anyone
could dream of claiming to be her

least of all the woman
there beside her
looking at that picture
which could not possibly be her

Kevin MacNeil

SILENCE IN THE MIRROR

Dermot Healy, *The Travels of Sorrow* (The Gallery Press, 2015), €11.95.

The Travels of Sorrow is published posthumously, following Dermot Healy's death at age 66 in June 2014. Healy was renowned as a novelist, memoirist, and playwright as well as a poet, and I think it's fair to say that there was a touch of poetry in everything he wrote – and, furthermore, that Healy was a poet at heart.

    The first book of his I read was the lyrical, autobiographical and imaginative *The Bend for Home* (1996). A number of impressions emerged from my reading of that book. For one thing, Healy crafted his sentences with extraordinary care – he was a writer's writer, if that phrase didn't imply exclusion. Healy's work had the winning mischievousness of Flann O'Brien as well as the dark existential humour of Samuel Beckett. There was the suggestion that Healy was a character, and a character of the kind that Celts seem to do so well: inordinately talented, humble, sensitive, simmering with humorous stories and an underlying melancholy ... The kind of person who might never quite achieve the acclaim he deserves.

    When I met Healy (appearing alongside him at a book festival in Aberdeen) he seemed every bit the Dermot Healy I expected. He was witty and relaxed and friendly, and there was something else about him, too, as if his inner life were fizzing over with important ideas, words, correspondences, images that wouldn't always let him be one hundred per cent present in the moment. I think this latter quality accounts for the sometimes hallucinatory quality in his writing. Indeed, in an interview with Sean O'Hagan, Healy said:

> I've experienced the odd hallucination of reality: out of nowhere comes the car that hits the bike. The feeling of: did that just happen? Or the bits of conversation that play in your head like a snatch of an old pop song that you can't get rid of. Hangovers can give you that feeling of an altered reality. And, maybe life ... is one big hangover.

Healy is a man who hears the whispering of shells, who finds silence in the mirror, who sees into the depth of things. His worldview is often perfectly humane and yet slightly askance – disconcerting, even. In a deliciously odd poem called 'The Off-button', he evokes a warmth and a chilliness at once:

> The ordinary
> I suddenly understand
> needs to go abroad.
> And the stranger
>
> needs to come home.
> I got this advice
> as moonlight
> whitened the stones.

The Travels of Sorrow generally gravitates around themes of ageing and death – and their attendant profundities and absurdities. There's also a great sense of kinship, of the importance of friendship and indeed of the bond that exists between humanity and nature. A number of the poems are elegies, hinting at vital words that were simply never said – an especially poignant subtext in a posthumous collection.

The title poem is characteristic. It tells the story of one Pat Donlon who, enraged at the height of an argument, took all the items of china from the house – vase, milk jug, plates – and dashed them to pieces on the rocks by the shore. Years afterwards, the narrator is building a stone wall and finds 'here a handle, / there a small flower // set in delph'. The poet understands that the 'thousand, thousand' high tides that have been and gone have sustained that old argument, bringing to the shore again and again 'the little fractures / of despair'. The ending is powerful in context:

> For years they've been going out
> and in with the tide.
>
> Sorrow never travels
> far from home.

This is classic Healy – bringing a luminous mind to bear on an ordinary tragedy and raising it to higher scrutiny. Here he sees meaning in the seemingly mundane, fixes it in a final devastating aphoristic couplet. (One of Healy's favourite techniques is to cadence his lines such that the endings unleash a powerful emotional wallop).

'Dry Eyes' similarly has a narrative that opens up sad truths. In seemingly chatty but beautifully measured lines, the poet describes a domestic cat that is blamed for his suffering from 'the dry eye'. The cat is banished outdoors:

> Every evening
>
> she tore the sea salt
> off the windows
> with her claws
>
> to watch us within.

When the cat dies in the dog kennel at nineteen, the poet comes to a realisation:

> But she was not to blame
> for whatever it was
> still burns my iris;
>
> my dry eyes continued
> after her death
> except on the day
>
> I buried her.

It's another small-scale tragedy that might be of no real consequence to anyone other than those immediately affected, but Healy explores, shares and evokes sorrow in such a way that a moving and lasting poem is the result. This is not to say that Healy deals exclusively with local events. 'En Route to Washington' takes on the subject of 9/11 in a manner that is unflinching, unsentimental and unforgettable:

> In the cockpit the final call to God
> was Muslim, down the aisles
> the last plea was mainly Christian,
>
> as both tribes
> balanced
> in the air
>
> for the final descent,
> face-down in the direction
> their prayers were sent.

The majority of these poems are emotionally engaging and thought-provoking. The sombre themes are occasionally leavened with humour or vignettes that have the grace and resonance of pub tales told by a storyteller of uncommon eloquence, empathy and insight. For all its darknesses, in other words, *The Travels of Sorrow* is an enriching and enjoyable read. Sometimes – very rarely – the author writes a poem that seems slight when weighed against the successes of the collection as a whole. For example, 'Fetch!' seems to me something of a throwaway (no pun intended) piece. Here it is in its entirety.

> If you want
> to break a dog's heart
> throw a stone
>
> into the sea.

That's more of a remark, an aside, than a poem. The other one that feels borderline flippant is 'Out There', which draws a parallel between 'a tall bowl of tall flowers' and a woman with

> ... head tilted forward,
> as she studies what's happening
> out there today.

So 'Out There' ends and so I am left wondering if I've missed something in the piece. Is it a poem of insularity intended, perhaps, to imply that the narrator feels scrutinized in a close-knit community? I don't know. I was left unmoved and that is why this poem and 'Fetch!' stand out in an otherwise quite remarkable collection. These poems feel insubstantial in comparison with more nuanced poems like 'The Mirror', which is about conjoined twins and can only have emerged from a mind that has as catalysts empathy, sympathy and sheer human decency. Not to mention brilliance. For I believe that Healy is a very fine poet indeed – maybe even one of Ireland's greatest writers of recent times. Whether bringing to life birdsong or silence ('Love, silence is the hardest song to sing'), presences or absences, personified moons or skeletons of trees, Healy is a poet of the visceral and the ineffable, both. Sometimes he writes in a manner that is intense, memorable, quotable ('Loneliness gathers. Here we are'). At its best, his writing achieves a marvellous synthesis of clarity and depth. The poem 'It Will Happen' features these lines:

> all the randomness
>
> peacefully random,
> the cows that will die
> looking out to sea,

> content, and what I will do
> now of little import:
> it will happen.

With *The Travels of Sorrow*, Healy packs so much life and death into his work that the reader feels mentally and emotionally enlarged for the reading of it. In a just world, this collection would be celebrated as a final gift from an enormously talented and underrated mind:

> ... the stones
> you're carrying to the ditch
> turn into tombs you'll be buried
> under one day.
> – 'THE SENTINEL'

For all its elegiac melancholy, *The Travels of Sorrow* is strangely uplifting; its morbidity is tempered by vitality. The second part of an elegy, 'The Fossils of Coral', ends:

> Seamus Slack was approaching ninety.
> He looked over at his son
> who was less than half his age.
>
> David, knowing he'd die first,
> took a drag of a fag, leaned over and tapped
> his father's arm, and said:
>
> 'Checkmate!'

John O'Donnell

POSTCARDS FROM THE EDGE

Anthony Cronin, *Body and Soul* (New Island Books), €13.99.
Enda Wyley, *Borrowed Space: New and Selected Poems* (Dedalus Press), €14.50.
Nessa O'Mahony, *Her Father's Daughter* (Salmon Poetry), €12.

In 'Writing', an early poem published in New Island's excellent *Collected Poems*, Cronin observes how 'In suffering we call out for another / Describing with a desperate precision.' The same 'desperate precision' is on view here in Cronin's latest collection. Almost fifty years ago in his magisterial *RMS Titanic*, Cronin heard the 'smooth hum' of money amid the clang and hammer of the shipyards, and this current collection shows Cronin's hearing is as acute as ever. The failure of the Oireachtas Banking Inquiry to ask Anthony Cronin to appear before it to give evidence was as much a missed opportunity as it was a failure of imagination: if you really want to find out what went wrong in this country over the past few years, Cronin's *Body and Soul* is a pungent, stirring litany of our failings. 'We are condemned to our temporal yearnings' he says ruefully in 'A Spiritual People', noting that while in the tweedy, sodden past we coveted 'That lovely coat in Monica Dowd's', in more recent times 'Dark limousines … White yachts … slender jet-planes' have been the less-than-obscure objects of our desire ('A Recession'). Cronin thunders against the avarice and greed of banks, but this book is far more than a soap-box rant against the latest pantomime villain. In 'Talking', Cronin observes just how we lost the run of ourselves; the lines could be a pithy summary of the property bubble: '… this is no time for the measured. / Everybody is floating on a tide / Of inspiration, malice, wrong / Information, misplaced enthusiasm'. His unflinching gaze perceives the human condition which has given rise to so much misery: 'Our most powerful concern: / Our self-esteem.' ('Memories of a Lifetime').

Perhaps the bar is set a bit too high for us, whether by ourselves or by some higher law. In 'The Supreme Commandment' Cronin wonders if we'd have been better off being urged to 'tolerate' rather than 'love' one another. He also muses on the existence – or otherwise – of the after-life: 'All that excitement, all that fear and pain / And then snuff out and never be again?' ('The Life of Man'). The collection is charged throughout with rhetoric, but these poems are made as much from the quarrel with ourselves as from the quarrel we have with others. Cronin's voice, formal, acerbic, dark and distinctive, is unlike that of any other writer in Ireland today.

The opening poem in *Body and Soul* recalls Wordsworth's encounter with 'The Lesser Spotted Celandine'. Larkin's mordant observation that 'deprivation is for me what daffodils were for Wordsworth' raises once more the question: does happiness write 'in white ink on a white page', as Henry de Montherlant put it?

Enda Wyley's *Borrowed Space: New and Selected Poems* challenges the assertion made by Clive James (among others) that art is an outward integration inspired by the artist's inner disintegration. This collection (a selection from four previous volumes as well as new material) is brimful with Wyley's warmth and zest for life. The opening lines of her early poem 'Municipal Gallery Favourite', dedicated to the now deceased Patrick Scott, are a fine example:

> I want to blow again
> down the fine straw
> of my childhood days
> that sunburst –
> huge orange gasp
> splattered on the canvas.

Many of the other early poems begin with 'I', though later works recognize the life – writing and otherwise – Wyley now shares with Peter Sirr: 'All the poems we might write, / gather here in these blank books' ('Notebook Shop'). A number of more recent poems are addressed tenderly to her daughter Freya: 'Little heart / not yet hurt / beat on.' ('Little Heart'). The poems eschew the political arena for the personal space instead; while 'Five Definitions of a Butterfly' is written after the end of the IRA ceasefire in 1996, Wyley more typically acknowledges her own good fortune instead of engaging with the plight of others: 'because of all these things / we know we are lucky / to rest here in our home' ('War'). In less assured hands the sweetness and positivity of her material could be cloying, but Wyley's excitement and lust for language is infectious – witness 'The Page Within', where she is inspired by the imminent birth of her daughter :'And the baby ripples within / pools of my safe, sweet water – / and this page that fills, filling fast.' Her affection for her home town is obvious, and many of the poems guide us through streets broad and narrow of Dublin's fair city. Wyley's poems are a life-affirming, joyful and engaging presence in our lives.

One of Wyley's poems, 'Postcard', is dedicated to the late Peter Porter, who wrote so movingly of very different postcards in his magnificent tribute to his late wife, 'An Exequy': 'A map of loss, some posted cards, / The living house reduced to shards, / The abstract hell of memory, / The pointlessness of poetry'. The heart of Nessa O'Mahony's collection, *Her Father's Daughter,* is a poignant and affecting series of reflections on the death of her own father. The book opens with 'Giving Me Away', an uneasy father and daughter road-trip which O'Mahony views initially as a sort of atonement by her father – 'Because you had never walked me down the aisle / you sit 330 miles in the passenger seat, / watching the speed-dial, / miming brakes' – as they head towards her 'new start' in Britain. However the tell-tale signs O'Mahony observes along the way reveal her father's decline: 'I know you've already / left me on this trip, / at Holyhead, at Dublin Port / before the ship embarked'. Later we are shown the agony – for relatives – of the slow death of a loved one: 'It has been a year / since you left / the hospital whites, / and were swallowed up / by your own chair' ('The Long Goodbye'). Elsewhere O'Mahony looks further back; in 'Walking Stick' the story of her grandfather's life is told by reference to his stick: 'An honest thing: / ash shaft, plain, / crook smooth' which has been 'Crafted to bear weight, / the tonnage of trench-foot', before being, 'Decommissioned once again / into night-watchman jobs / in Coventry, in Cricklewood.' A cane is visible in the striking cover photograph of the same grandfather 'kitted out as the pride / of the Munster Fusiliers' ('Casting Lots'), in which poem O'Mahony also hints intriguingly at the choice facing her grandfather and his brother: 'who'd go, / who'd return / to farm and family'. At times O'Mahony feels guilty writing about the illnesses and deaths of loved ones. In 'His Master's Voice' dedicated to the late James Simmons, she considers Simmons's elderly dog Charlie on the day his master's coffin is carried out: 'He can't know that a stranger / will come soon, tidying, / sweeping up, thieving a poem / like a starving cur grabs a bone / where she finds it.'

'Portrait of the Artist's Father' is really a portrait of the artist writing about her father's illness 'I trawl for metaphors, / imagine corollaries / for the fluid filling your lungs', before acknowledging the perceived impropriety of so doing:

> My page
> has been empty
> for months.
> Forgive me
> for filling it.

O'Mahony should not reproach herself: Graham Greene's famous insight that there is 'a splinter of ice in the heart of a writer' came to him in hospital, as he listened to and watched from a nearby bed the tears and cries of a mother whose son had just died, thinking: 'This is something which one day I might need.' A writer does need a good editor, however, and there are a couple of curious glitches in an otherwise attractive presentation. A more ruthless editor might also have advised against the inclusion of one or two less successful pieces. At its best, though, O'Mahony's forthright, heartfelt style is affecting, and further exploration of her family hinterland will no doubt yield up other secrets.

Michael Longley

IN THE MUGELLO

I
It is the nightingale's
Mugello melody
Above the parasol
That brings us together,
Old friends and new, to dine
On aubergines – perfect
Circles – and zucchini,
Heidi's speciality.
A nervy doe steps out
From the wood, then her fawn.

II
Lorenzo renovates
His antique radios,
Tightening valves and fine-
Tuning signals world-wide
From those who have dreamed here
Beneath the elbow-shaped
Roof-beams, honeymooners,
Weary farm-labourers,
The likes of me fiddling
With childhood's crystal set.

III
We are too late, my love,
For the lizard orchids
Already intertwined
In Silvano's hay-bales.
But then you discover
Survivors, harvest's soul,
Four under a hornbeam,
Other orchids as well
Decorating the verge,
Pyramids, labia-pink.

Michael Longley

KINDLING

We walk to the waterfall
And firefly memories
On the longest day, past
Elvira's weedy terrace
And the dilapidated mill,
Through brambles and goosegrass
Tangles, adder-alert, you
(Who as a child, you say,
Arranged in an egg cup
Buttercups and daisies)
Too late for orchids now
Picking angelica, cow
Parsley, scabious, wild pea,
While I, too soon for sloes
Or elderberries, gather
Winter kindling, and you
Offer me your nosegay and
Egg cup like a chalice.

Michael Longley

THE CHESTNUT PAN

Sunlight through chestnut leaves
Conjures at the waterfall
That jar of chestnut honey
On the kitchen table
And the griddle full of holes
For roasting chestnuts – wet
Towels around hands and shins –
Ember constellations
Beside the waterfall,
The smoky chestnut pan.

Eiléan Ní Chuilleanáin

PERFUME

Ed. by Richard Zenith, 28 *Portuguese Poets: A Bilingual Anthology*, translated by Richard Zenith and Alexis Levitin (Dedalus Press, 2015), €14.99.
Antonella Anedda, *Archipelago*, translated by Jamie McKendrick (Bloodaxe Books, 2015), £12.
René Char, *Hypnos*, translated by Mark Hutchinson (Seagull Books, 2014), hb $21.

John Donne wrote about exotic, imported perfumes and unimpressed Englishmen:

> … we in our Ile imprisoned
> Where cattle onely, and divers dogs are bred,
> The precious Unicorns, strange monsters, call …

Well, in linguistic terms we are not imprisoned in our island. The English language, like the ocean that bore the Eastern carracks of Donne's day, delivers treasure from many quarters to publishers in England and Ireland and further away; the navigators are the translators with their combined skill in understanding and reframing – but there are still readers whose welcome is at best qualified. Some are impatient when presented with translated poems, unwilling to be seduced by the strange; while others may suspect the commodity is adulterated, and cavil at perceived inaccuracies. A recent spat between the distinguished translator Michael Hofmann and a reader who looked for precise equivalences in his versions of Gottfried Benn has led Hofmann to denounce the habit of printing the originals and translations on facing pages – suggesting it is better if the reader is shielded from the temptation to scrutinize and from the search for equivalences invited by the bilingual volume when the reader has some linguistic competence.

Since the internet came on us we have realized, just by the contrast, some of the physical impact of a poem as a thing held in the hand, and of the slight but definite weightiness of a collection of poems. Slim or substantial, we can navigate back and forth in a bound book, planting a finger or a gas bill as a marker, pouncing and postponing. (Some poems will be read repeatedly, in the light of others; some only once as we register where they fit in a pattern we are making out). A bilingual volume with facing pages invites a special gaze. Everyone's grasp of languages differs, especially at the borderlines where we rub up against incomprehension. All reading that is not spelling out involves a rapid succession of guesses, and in a foreign language (that we think we know) we continue to guess; we stumble about as in a half-lit room, stubbing our toes on unfamiliar obstacles in the gloom and comforting ourselves with the dictionary.

In these three volumes I encounter three different experiences: I read French regularly, I frequently read, write and speak in Italian and translate from it, and have in fact translated some poems by one of the authors I am reviewing, Antonella Anedda; but I merely assent to a translation from Portuguese as I catch the echoes from the other Romance languages. In both Jamie McKendrick's Anedda and Richard Zenith and Alexis Levitin's versions of Portuguese poets I find I am grateful for the publisher's generosity in printing the originals even though my ability to judge the translations on the fidelity score differs so widely.

The twenty-eight Portuguese poets are in fact twenty-five, since the first four are all voices of Fernando Pessoa, works he published under his own name and under his notorious 'heteronyms'. What a gift to the poetic history of the Portuguese twentieth century, to start with such a phalanx. Pessoa invented those variegated personae, but among the actually historical personages whose voices we encounter here there is as it were a continuity of variety: in origins (from the mother country, and the island and African colonies, Madeira, Angola, Mozambique – the vastness of Brazil would be another story); and variety also evident in lifestyle, with scholars, monks, wild women, mothers, political agitators among them. For me the pleasure of discovery meant too recognizing once more the genius of Pessoa, as well as tracing the maritime themes that surface in so many poets, and being overwhelmed by a sensory assault from Herberto Helder:

> ... thumbs plunging to where the orange
> swiftly thinks, and develops, and annihilates, and then
> is reborn ...
> ... I write
> a song to have knowledge about fruits
> on the tongue, in subtle canals, down
> to a dark emotion.
> – 'SEATED THEORY' (II), ZENITH'S TRANSLATION

Passion and need surface also in the work of Fiama Hasse Pais Brandão:

> I bore through the ground to make way
> for the mole. It climbs up. It dances
> with fire. I give the remainder of my experiences
> to animals. I break bread with
> Euripides ...
> – 'I BORE THROUGH THE GROUND TO MAKE WAY', LEVITIN'S TRANSLATION

Perhaps it is just that these translators are drawn to the dynamic energy of certain poets. The editor apologizes for exclusions, and everyone who is aware of anthologies' limitations will know he must be right. But within the boundaries of a substantial volume he gives generous selections and one does feel that it's been possible to make new acquaintances, almost friendships with the poets that have attracted him and his colleagues.

Antonella Anedda grew up among a clutch of languages, principally standard Italian (she was born in Rome), and the Sardinian language Logudorese which she heard spoken during long periods spent in the island of La Maddalena off the Sardinian coast, where her parents came from. In this volume we have her originals, including some in Logudorese. One of these is a telling act of revenge on the Roman empire, as she translates the Latin eloquence of Cicero (in a speech defending the corrupt governor of the island against his native accusers) – how could one believe a word from these lying people, from a place where 'even honey is gall'. In their own language, in many ways closer to Latin than the great official tongues: 'Zente chene ide ... terra ue peri su mele est 'ele' ('Contro Scaurum'; the ellipsis is hers).

This is a fine account of her work. I find the liberties McKendrick takes in translation quite justifiable, even in places where I might take different liberties myself. If he offers 'the see-saw life of the ward' instead of 'the fluctuating life of the hospital' which is closer to the literal meaning [in 'Chorus (for my mother)'], it is because in reading he has become inflamed with vision, he is actually seeing the hospital ward. If he has included fewer than I had hoped of the marvellous, spare pieces in Anedda's most recent volume *Salva con nome / Save As*, he has given the reader a strong sense of her development over three decades, and in particular of how she has developed her homage to the doomed Amelia Rosselli and cleared a space in which her own, less agitated, more weighty voice could emerge. Her later poems draw attention to absences, to half-apprehended shapes, like the vacated marks of furniture that has been moved away, for whatever sad reason; the suitcase packed for an uncertain future, the resolve that is steady rather than frantic. McKendrick has included a group of prose meditations on paintings taken from a book where they were originally accompanied by illustrations; the translator intervenes, then, not merely by selecting what to translate but by re-arranging the work in ways that redirect attention: another kind of fidelity.

The Portuguese anthology surveys a national and colonial literature over almost a century, the Italian book a notable poetic career over thirty years. Mark Hutchinson's translation of René Char's *Feuillets d'Hypnos* is a brief clip out of a long and celebrated writing life, and out of the history of the second world war in France. The title in French, and the translator's labelling of the pieces as 'Fragments', tell us to expect scraps and jottings from a time of great pressures as the author (code-named Capitaine Alexandre) led a group of Resistance fighters in the Alps in 1943-44. Thus not to expect coherence. But the presence of a mythic persona, Hypnos, points to the poet's imaginative licence; thus warns us not to expect accuracy. His brief prose observations are apocalyptic, energetic, impatient and reflect the actuality of a time of struggle. Even accounts where important details have been changed have the authenticity of a mind under pressure imagining its own responses and calculations. We know, from other writings of René Char himself, that he did not witness the shooting of a comrade and fellow poet, Roger Bernard; but in Fragment 138 he imagines himself 'some hundred yards away', with enough companions to take on the SS, and decides that he could not give the order to intervene as the Germans would have taken revenge on the civilian population of the locality. Constantly braced, thinking into a future tense, preoccupied with the discipline which will enable him and his men to 'do the job properly and see it through to the end' (Fragment 76) he experiences 'not fear, just vertigo' (Hutchinson has 'I'm not frightened, merely giddy'; [48]). He celebrates friendship, solidarity, responsibility, which bind him to his group of Maquisards and create a distance from others, peasants and women for example, so sometimes they might belong to a different species.

The poet-persona Hypnos enables these refractions of experience. The succession of fragments suggests the chaotic conditions of their writing, in a notebook which was copied out when the war was over, while also exemplifying a poetic credo that saw poetry as a disturbing, a dislocating energy. Fragment 203 expresses it: 'I was a hive flying off to the springs of altitude with all its honey and bees on board'. In 178, he rejoices to find that the eyes of new recruits to the group 'smart' at the troubling beauty of a reproduction of a painting by his beloved Georges de la Tour.

While I had to check with the Gallimard edition of Char's poetry of 1962, in order to see how the translator had expanded 'un colt' into 'a Colt 45' (50), or made 'Discipline, comme tu saignes' into 'Discipline, you're bleeding all over!' (40), I was not impelled by any desire to hunt down imperfect correspondences. What I was finding is how the impulse to translate is also an impulse to rewrite, one that is held in check but is discernible constantly in these small and justifiable variations. This is how we read poetry, constantly remaking it in our heads, aware of the writer and his careful selections in his own language. The bilingual edition shows us the translator too selecting, creating almost involuntarily but necessarily a new poem.

Klinë / Klina, Kosovo, June 1999 © **Seamus Murphy**

Kabul, Afghanistan, October 2007 © **Seamus Murphy**

Mitrovicë / Mitrovica, Kosovo, July 1999 © **Seamus Murphy**

Kabul, Afghanistan, November 2002 © **Seamus Murphy**

HISTORY AND MAGIC: SEAMUS MURPHY IN CONVERSATION WITH NELL REGAN

I met up with photographer and film maker Seamus Murphy to talk poetry and photography for *Poetry Ireland Review*, on the eve of the launch of *The Hollow of The Hand* (Bloomsbury Circus), his collaboration with singer-songwriter and poet, PJ Harvey.

Called a 'poet with a camera', Seamus Murphy has garnered seven World Press Photo awards for his work in Afghanistan, Sierra Leone, Gaza, Lebanon, Peru, Ireland and England. His first book, *Afghanistan: A Darkness Visible:* (Saqi Books, 2008), is a collection of his images chronicling the life of the Afghan people, and it won the World Understanding Award from Pictures of the Year International. His second, *I Am the Beggar of the World: Landays from Contemporary Afghanistan* (Farrar, Straus and Giroux, 2014) is a collaboration with US poet and journalist Eliza Griswold. The pair worked undercover to collect these two-line Pashtun folk poems which are composed and recited by Afghani women in secret. Eliza Griswold was awarded the 2015 PEN Award for Poetry in Translation for the collection.

Murphy is also an award-winning filmmaker, and initially worked with PJ Harvey making *12 Short Films* for her album *Let England Shake*. *The Hollow of The Hand* is his third book and he is currently finishing a new collection of Irish photographs, *The Republic,* due out in March 2016 with Allen Lane (Penguin Books).

Nell Regan: Your two latest books, *Beggar of the World* and *Hollow of The Hand*, are both photography and poetry collaborations – what has drawn you to these? Why poetry?

Seamus Murphy: In some ways it was down to circumstances, but what isn't? The landay project was the result of an idea I had of doing something with Eliza on the modernist Afghan poet Sayd Bahodine Majrouh. I hadn't read any of his poetry, but I came across him in the book *Songs of Love and War: Afghan Women's Poetry (*Other Press, 2003), a book of landays that he and his sister gathered from refugees in Pakistan during the Soviet invasion of Afghanistan.

Just reading about him was enough to interest and excite me. He was something of a bohemian, an enigmatic and learned man – the sort of intellectual that Afghanistan needs and has long needed but that has been lost through war and exile. He was assassinated on his doorstep in Peshawar by the mujahideen, his fellow Afghans, for warning the refugees against the fundamentalism he predicted would fester in a liberated Afghanistan.

Anyway, that led on to reading the landays in *Songs of Love and War* and being completely knocked out by their brave, raw, earthy, honesty. So we decided we should try and further his and his sister's search by finding and preserving more landays. [*Their first landay trip was an assignment for the* New York Times, *in search of the identity of Muska, a 15 year old who had committed suicide after being punished for writing landays*].

The PJ Harvey collaboration had a number of elements – poetry, photography, an album and a film and it evolved from working together. I had made *Let England Shake: 12 Short Films* after she had written and recorded the songs. Polly had started to write poetry seriously, and this time we decided that we would grow the next project together, from the beginning. She wanted to continue writing about the wider world and needed more exposure to that, so we travelled together – to Kosovo, Afghanistan and Washington DC.

NR: There is a wonderful phrase used about the landays project – 'investigative poetry'.

SM: Yes, what's interesting is the reporting/journalistic aspect of both collaborations. Eliza is a renowned journalist as well as poet and she utilized both to achieve her work in *Beggar of the World*. In her introduction, she says we joked about creating this new genre of poetry, *investigative poetry*.

Polly wanted to be a poet/songwriter/reporter. In an interview on *Front Row*, the BBC Radio 4 arts programme, she mused on being appointed an official war-songwriter, like a commissioned war-artist. 'I'd relish it,' she said. What was funny was that we were planning to do some travels but were being very careful not to tell anyone. There are UK correspondents there and obviously it would have been a great story, as she had just won her second Mercury. We had to keep it very discreet.

NR: Were they different from other collaborations you have done?

SM: I think there is more equality in the collaboration with poetry. It might be to do with poems and photos standing alone, able to exist without the other, or with the nature of poetry and so called 'poetic licence'. Working in journalism is about information: that isn't wanted or expected of poetry. There is a tendency – understandably – to link slavishly the words with the pictures. The pictures illustrate the words and the words tend to caption the picture, when in actuality, even if it's of the same event, they are made in two separate worlds, captured by two different individuals and at different times. The photograph was taken at 3.27

p.m., the writer makes a note around that time but at 7.45 that night or two weeks later, writes about it. The newspaper or magazine merges the two into a seamless unity but it is all in hindsight. This is far more real ... far more true because they *are* different things. We're standing in the same place, but to try and put them together and make them units? It is better to separate them and find what's common rather than match one to one.

NR: Where then for you do poetry and photography 'meet', or what is the relationship?

SM: I think poetry does naturally ally itself with photography and vice-versa. It's the capture, a moment that stands for eternity, a gesture that sums up a life or is just that, a gesture.

NR: CD Wright, the US poet who has collaborated with several photographers, comments that, 'There is in the very bone of collaborating, a willingness to make mistakes. After all no one is in total control.' I love this and wondered if you'd tell us a bit about how you worked with Eliza and Polly.

SM: I love mistakes – it's probably why I don't have much time for conceptual photography! You bump into things and I think the cleverness is in being able to use it rather than saying, 'Well I didn't intend that so I am not going to use it.' I think that's po-faced.

I have to say that although both projects are collaborations, we still worked individually on our own crafts. With *Beggar of the World,* there were a lot of logistics that required Eliza's and my attention. We were travelling in some very hostile places – Nangarhar and Helmand Province – and working on a project most considered taboo, so it presented a myriad of challenges we had to deal with together. The collaborations were more in decision-making, and the execution and production of the finished book.

In the design and layout of *Hollow*, we very deliberately separated the poetry from the photography, so both could have their voice and not be too closely associated with the other. We didn't want – here's a poem about an old woman and here's her photograph. The photographs are forensic enough in that they are unstaged, and documentary, have a place name and a date provided. I would always want them to transcend that information, to go beyond the mere *reality.*

NR: Was there much informal or incidental cross fertilisation or did you find you were influenced by the way the poets worked?

SM: We all work in different ways. The biggest influence is often the discussion and understanding we get from each other after experiencing something together; themes emerge. We might tell each other about something we had noticed, which the other person hadn't or hadn't given much thought to, which can play into how we view things and that influences what follows.

NR: Are there any particular examples of this from your travels with PJ Harvey?

SM: We spent half an hour in this abandoned village in Kosovo and discovered later, when talking about it, that the exact same two things really struck us. This woman lived there among the abandoned houses and as she was walking in front of us she had these keys behind her back – I had filmed them and also rotting plums in this pathway, flies buzzing, rotting because no one had picked them. There were so many things that could have struck us, but that was really interesting, that they were the same two things.

    The other thing was a Sufi ceremony we went to in Afghanistan. They were very welcoming and as they were Sufis, it was no problem for a woman to come in. It is very impressive, the audio is amazing and when their chanting reaches a climax, there's a guy in the background who starts praying, then it continues and builds up again. Polly had been taking notes and afterwards said, 'I think they're trying to burrow into the earth and find out what is going on.' She had made this drawing, like a spiral and it was wonderful because I'd always be thinking about what photographs I could get – about positions, about this, that and the other, everything obviously for pictures, so it's got to be tangible, it's got to be physical ... superficial in some ways. But because she's a writer she can think about this ... I couldn't photograph a man and make the same thing live. It was such a fresh thing for me – I mean I had been to this place about ten times and it was something I had never ever thought. That for me was wonderful.

NR: So, for *Hollow*, how long did you actually spend travelling together?

SM: Kosovo was four days, Afghanistan was a week and DC was two weeks. After the first trip to Kosovo she spent six months working on the material (she was doing other stuff as well).

NR: Are your photographs in the book all from those trips with PJ Harvey?

SM: No! I had to go back to my archive unless I was to go back physically. And there are so many places I have been that are impossible now. As a photographer you have to keep this archive otherwise it's always difficult.

NR: I hadn't thought about it in that sense – it is such an interesting (and now that you say it, obvious!) difference – that as a writer you can keep mining the experience or trip.

SM: Huge difference. That's the thing about writing – you can spend five minutes here and then go off for a week or a day and work on it. With photography – what you walk away with is what you walk away with.

NR: So after the Kosovo trip did you meet up and exchange 'manuscripts' or how did it work?

SM: I would send her pictures, audio and video from the trip and that might reinforce things she'd written about. She's very specific (and famous for that) so she had already worked out what she wanted. Anything else would be extra work or distraction. We would to and fro on e-mail, on the phone and meet up for a drink and she would send me some poems, but not that much. She was working a lot with Don Paterson, so was holding stuff back till she got that out of the way.

NR: You did mention being detained on that trip and earlier talked about the risk involved in the landays project. Were there any times that you felt in serious danger?

SM: Working with Eliza was a lot more intense in terms of where we were going. Plus, she was five months pregnant. We went to meet a Governor who was very interested that we were following the story of Muska and that we had found her grave. He provided security to get us to his Palace – Eliza was told to put a burka on and I was hiding in the back seat. There is only one road so if you go out to it ... they know you're coming back. Next thing this guy in a tuk-tuk is coming right up to us, we hit him and of course the crowd gathers. They're all looking in and our cover is blown, I thought I might as well get up and take pictures. I really thought it was a suicide bomber come to blow us up ... but he was just an idiot! We were there for an hour – so, do we go home? They're all taking photos and on their mobiles to who knows who – so, *do we go on*? Well, we went on. It could have been the end for us – there was an IED [*Improvised Explosive Device*] attack that day on that road – maybe for us? And if anything had happened people would have said it was stupidity on our part, that, 'you shouldn't have done it'. And of course you *shouldn't* have done it, but then you wouldn't have got the poem, the image, the story.

NR: Could you tell us a bit more about the process of gathering the landays and photographing the process?

SM: Because of the restrictions of photographing women in Afghanistan – especially in the rural Pashtun areas where those codes are strictly enforced – I ended up photographing the world that Afghan women lived in and saw, rather than focus so much on individuals and their faces.

In the end, in the context of hearing the women speaking themselves, it was more meaningful to actually see what they were speaking about. Also the anonymous, taboo nature of landays meant that revealing identities was counter to the spirit of landays. Eliza spent a huge amount of time working with translators to find the right words to convey the meaning of the landays.

On one occasion at a camp in Kabul, I was working outside and she was interviewing a man and his three wives. He was a bit of a character and boastful and she got him to allow me come into their home in the camp. Eliza said the women – one in particular – who with her had been very strong, forceful and outspoken characters, covered up as soon as I walked in and turned mute. It was interesting for her to see the transformation but also it made us realize it was counterproductive to try and have me more present during the poetry gathering process.

NR: What did you most enjoy about the collaborations?

SM: Working with someone else for a change. It can be a lonely old calling being a photographer (I bet Eliza and Polly would say the same about being a poet).

NR: You've actually been called 'a poet with a camera'? Could you tell us a bit about the context of that?

SM: Yes, it was lovely to hear. That was Philip Jones Griffiths [*renowned photojournalist, author of* Vietnam Inc.] who was Welsh. He liked my work from Afghanistan, calling it humanistic and poetic. I think he appreciated that it was about the Afghans when so much of the coverage of Afghanistan at that time was about the American, British and NATO forces and their stories. He'd be into poetry, he was a literary 'sort'.

NR: It does strike me about your photographs – how you manage to capture opposites and incongruous things ...

SM: As you say, it's what we leave out … and it's one reason I like poetry – that economy. Up until doing this Irish book I'd been filming, and then to go back to photography is quite a discipline. It is so near to poetry. There are so many things you don't have, you don't have audio or movement. It is that one image, it's there. You have to get used to it again, to re-enter it.

NR: Where did you learn your own craft of photography?

SM: I just picked it up. I was living in San Francisco and painting houses after college. I was always interested in photography but never really had the time, or the resources, as a student in Dublin to develop it. I went to America and there was a dark room, a public dark room, nearby, and that's what got me into it. Then there were these yard sales, people selling whole record and book collections and I was buying photography books which I wouldn't have been able to get that easily in Ireland and I learned a lot from that.

NR: Who did you like or who were your influences?

SM: There'd be some stuff I wouldn't particularly like – like landscapes, I found that quite boring, but I'd buy them. I loved Cartier-Bresson, Gilles Peress, André Kertész, Lartigue, Lee Friedlander … I didn't come across Robert Frank till years later, but I'd have loved him. The old masters really and then odd stuff, photographers you would never have heard of. Seeing someone doing something niche (like our publications), made you realize, someone bothers to print this. For years I was a photojournalist but always did my own stuff and that's what I love to do most. I am doing more now and feel I am back to the way I started out. It's sort of intuitive … It's poetic in a way too because you're not thinking about the market or the form or the story … The story *is* the picture. It's the thing in itself.

NR: Back to that, and where poetry and photography meet really…

SM: Absolutely and what I love about poetry is the … well, it's almost like a punch line. It's often at the very end (but it doesn't always have to be) and it's that blinding … epiphany that you get …

NR: The aha …

SM: Exactly. It can be slowly built up and then *bang* and *that's* like the shutter. It really is the decisive moment, but the interesting thing about poetry, about writing, is that you can refine it, fashion it. I know from writing my own bits of prose that you write something and then think, if I put that there it's better, stronger. You edit the stuff – I guess with poetry too? Yes. That makes sense, you have this 'punch line' and you might think, I'm going to build it up later and I love that, and again it's that process which you can't do with photography, where you are completely hostage to fortune.

NR: But don't you have to have built up such a level of craft and the ability to know when ... ?

SM: I think that's true but it's such a bloody physical thing! You have to *literally* dart across the room to get that picture or you've got to climb on a chair *immediately* because if you don't, the cat that's about to do something will have jumped and you won't be able to see it against the green wall in a way that makes the best picture – so you've just got to jump up on a chair. You have to be physically present and it's physically demanding. The difference between a great picture and an ordinary picture could be just ducking down, it could be just the position of your body.

NR: And do you know when you've taken a photograph if it works?

SM: Yeah, you know.

NR: You've described photography as 'part history, part magic'.

SM: Every photograph is history, every photograph is the past, you can't repeat it so whatever else a photograph is or can be – it is an historic document.
 The magic is the indefinable element of what it is that is a photograph, or that which makes a good photograph. If we knew really what it was you could turn it on, but you can't. You think *it's simple mechanical recording and it's not like writing or painting* ... but it *is* and the most interesting photograph reveals the thoughts and concerns of the photographer. If you're not in the mood, you don't get the pictures. That's alchemy and that's poetry – and that's where the magic comes in.

Notes on Contributors

Paul Batchelor was born in Northumberland. His first full-length collection of poems, *The Sinking Road*, was published by Bloodaxe Books in 2008, and in 2014 Clutag published his chapbook, *The Love Darg*. He is a lecturer in English Literature and Creative Writing at Durham University.

Tara Bergin is from Dublin. Her first collection, *This is Yarrow*, was published by Carcanet in 2013, and was awarded the Seamus Heaney Centre for Poetry Prize, and the Irish Shine/Strong Award for best first collection by an Irish author. She currently lives in the North of England.

Ciaran Berry's collections *The Sphere of Birds* (2008) and *The Dead Zoo* (2013) are published by The Gallery Press.

Beverley Bie Brahic is a Canadian who lives in France. Her poetry collection *White Sheets* (CB Editions, 2012) was a finalist for the Forward Prize, and her translation of Apollinaire, *The Little Auto* (CB Editions, 2012), was awarded the 2014 Scott Moncrieff Prize. Her most recent translation is Yves Bonnefoy, *The Anchor's Long Chain* (Seagull Books, 2015).

Paddy Bushe is a prize-winning poet in Irish and in English. His collections include *Poems With Amergin* (1989), *Digging Towards The Light* (1994), *In Ainneoin na gCloch* (Coiscéim, 2001), and *The Nitpicking of Cranes* (2004). *To Ring in Silence: New and Selected Poems* was published by Dedalus Press in 2008. He edited the anthology *Voices at the World's Edge: Irish Poets on Skellig Michael* (Dedalus Press, 2010). His latest collection is *My Lord Buddha of Carraig Eanna* (Dedalus Press, 2012). He is a member of Aosdána.

David Butler's collection *Via Crucis* was published by Doghouse Books in 2011. His latest novel, *City of Dis* (New Island Books, 2014), was shortlisted for the Kerry Group Irish Novel of the Year 2015.

John Wedgwood Clarke's first full poetry collection *Ghost Pot* was published in 2013 by Valley Press. His forthcoming collection centres on a landfill site. He is a lecturer in Creative Writing and Literature at the University of Hull.

Henri Cole was born in Fukuoka, Japan. He has published nine collections of poetry, including *Middle Earth* (Farrar, Straus and Giroux, 2003), which was a finalist for the Pulitzer Prize in Poetry. He has received many awards for his work, including the Jackson Prize, the Kingsley Tufts Award, the Rome Prize, the Berlin Prize, a Guggenheim Fellowship, and the Lenore Marshall Award. His most recent collection, *Nothing to Declare*, was published by Farrar, Straus and Giroux in 2015. He lives in Boston.

Lucy Collins is a lecturer at University College, Dublin, where she teaches modern poetry. Her most recent book, *Contemporary Irish Women Poets: Memory and Estrangement*, was published by Liverpool University Press in September 2015.

Enda Coyle-Greene's first collection, *Snow Negatives*, won the Patrick Kavanagh Award in 2006 and was published by Dedalus Press in 2007. Her second collection, *Map of the Last*, also from Dedalus Press, was published in 2013.

Ellen Cranitch's poems are published by Carcanet in the Oxford Poets series. Her work has appeared in a range of magazines including *Poetry London*, *Poetry Wales* and *Ambit*, and has won numerous awards, including prizes in the Poetry London, Troubadour International and South Bank Poetry Competitions.

Armel Dagorn lives in France, having lived for seven years in Ireland. His writing has appeared in magazines such as *The Rialto*, *The Stinging Fly*, *The Penny Dreadful* and *THE SHOp*, and he won the 2014 Bailieborough Poetry Prize. He is working on a first collection.

Patrick Deeley's *Groundswell: New and Selected Poems* is the latest of his six collections with Dedalus Press. His awards include the Eilís Dillon Award and the Dermot Healy Poetry Prize. His memoir, *The Hurley-Maker's Son*, is due for publication by Doubleday Ireland in 2016.

Martina Evans, poet and novelist, was born in Cork, the youngest of ten children. She is the author of ten books of poetry and prose. *Facing the Public* (Anvil Poetry, 2012) was a *TLS* Book of the Year and recipient of the Premio Piero Ciampi Prize for Poetry. *Burnfort, Las Vegas* (Anvil Press, 2014) was short-listed for the *Irish Times* Poetry Now Award (2015).

Emer Fallon writes poetry and fiction. Her poetry has appeared in *The SHOp*, *The Stinging Fly* and *The Poetry Bus*, and has been shortlisted for the Bridport Prize, Listowel Writers' Week poetry collection competition, and the Fish Poetry Prize. She lives in West Kerry with her husband and two daughters.

Tom French's collections, *Touching the Bones* (2001), *The Fire Step* (2009) and *Midnightstown* (2014), are published by The Gallery Press. A new e-chapbook, *Taking the Oath*, appeared from www.smithereenspress.com in the spring of 2015.

Frances Galleymore lives on the south-east coast of England. Her poems have been published in *Acumen*, *Orbis*, *South Bank Poetry*, and in the Ver Prize and Templar Awards anthologies. She won the Battered Moons Poetry Competition and was shortlisted for the Keats-Shelley Prize. She is also a novelist.

Mary Melvin Geoghegan has four collections of poetry published, most recently *Say it Like a Paragraph* (Bradshaw Books, 2012). Her work has been published in *Poetry Ireland Review*, *The SHop*, *The Oxfam Calendar*, *The Moth*, *The Stinging Fly*, *Crannóg*, *Skylight 47*, and elsewhere. A member of Poetry Ireland's Writers in Schools Scheme, she has edited several anthologies of Longford children's poetry. She won the Longford Festival Award for Poetry (2013) and was shortlisted for the Cúirt New Writing Prize 2015.

Alan Gillis is from Belfast, and teaches English Literature at The University of Edinburgh. His new book *Scapegoat* (2014) follows *Here Comes the Night* (2010), both published by The Gallery Press. He was chosen by the Poetry Book Society as a 'Next Generation Poet' in 2014.

Desmond Graham's most recent collection is *The Scale of Change* (Flambard Press, 2011), and pamphlets from the Villa Vic Press, 'Unaccompanied' and 'Brain Songs' (first published in Polish translation as 'Nowe Wiersze', Gdansk 2014). He is a biographer of Keith Douglas, and Emeritus Professor of Poetry at Newcastle.

Kevin Graham was Featured Poet in the summer 2014 issue of *The Stinging Fly*. Recent poems have appeared in *Oxford Poetry*, *Agenda* and *Poetry Salzburg Review*. He was shortlisted for a 2014 Hennessy Literary Award and is working towards his first collection.

Joanna Guthrie's first collection, *Billack's Bones*, was published by *The Rialto* in 2007. In 2014 she was one of eight emerging poets chosen for the Poetry Trust's Aldeburgh Eight development programme.

Jared Harel was awarded the 2015 Stanley Kunitz Memorial Prize from the *American Poetry Review*. Additionally, his poems have appeared in such journals as *Tin House*, *The Threepenny Review*, *The Southern Review*, *Shenandoah* and *Ecotone*. His chapbook, *The Body Double*, was published by Brooklyn Arts Press. A graduate of Cornell's MFA program, he lives in Queens, NY and plays drums in the twang-rock band, The Dust Engineers.

Maurice Harmon, a former editor of *Poetry Ireland Review*, is a poet, scholar and critic who taught at University College, Dublin for many years. He has just published *Hoops of Holiness* (Salmon Poetry), his sixth collection. He is preparing a book of essays on Irish poetry after Seamus Heaney.

Libby Hart is an Australian poet. Her collections include *Fresh News from the Arctic* (2006), *This Floating World* (2011) and *Wild* (2014). *Wild* was named one of the Books of the Year 2014 for the *Australian Book Review*, *The Age* and *The Sydney Morning Herald*. See **libbyhartfile.blogspot.com**.

Kevin Higgins's poems feature in *Identity Parade: New British and Irish Poets* (Bloodaxe Books, 2010), and in *The Hundred Years' War: Modern War Poems* (Bloodaxe Books, 2014), edited by Neil Astley. His fourth collection of poems, *The Ghost In The Lobby*, was published by Salmon Poetry in 2014.

Michael Longley, born in Belfast, was Ireland Professor of Poetry from 2007 to 2010. He has published many collections of his work, among them *Gorse Fires* (Wake Forest Press, 1991), which won the Whitbread Poetry Prize, and *The Weather in Japan* (Wake Forest Press, 2000), which won the TS Eliot Prize and the Hawthornden Prize. He was the 2001 recipient of the Queen's Gold Medal for Poetry. His most recent collection, *The Stairwell* (Cape Poetry, 2014), received the Griffin International Poetry Prize.

Annabel Luery has been published in *New Voices* (Shoestring Press, 2000), which was commissioned by East Midland Arts and features three poets, and in *Saltings* (Shoestring Press, 2001), a chapbook sequence. She is returning to writing following a lengthy gap due to illness.

Alice Lyons's latest collection, *The Breadbasket of Europe*, will be published next year by Veer Books, London. Born in Paterson, New Jersey, and living in Sligo and Roscommon since 1998, she is currently a Fellow in poetry at the Radcliffe Institute for Advanced Study, Harvard University.

Kevin MacNeil is originally from the Outer Hebrides and is an award-winning poet, novelist, lyricist and scriptwriter. His novel *The Brilliant & Forever* is forthcoming from Polygon in 2016. A practising Buddhist, he currently lives in London. See **KevinMacNeil.com**.

Luke Morgan has poems published in *Poetry Ireland Review*, *Poetry Review* (UK), the *Irish Independent*, *Cyphers* and *Crannóg* among other magazines. He lives in Galway.

John Murphy's collection, *The Book of Water*, was published by Salmon Poetry. He is the winner of the 2015 Strokestown International Poetry Prize.

Ceaití Ní Bheildiúin: Tá a ceathrú cnuasacht filíochta idir lámha ag Ceaití. Fuair sí sparántacht ó Ealaín na Gaeltachta i 2014. *Meirge an Laoich* (Coiscéim, 2013) is ea an cnuasach filíochta is déanaí óna peann. Tá Duais Foras na Gaeilge 2015 buaite aici leis an dán 'Sanas sa Ghob Daortha'.

Eiléan Ní Chuilleanáin is a poet and translator from Irish, Italian and Romanian. She still teaches at Trinity College Dublin after her retirement in 2011. She is one of the founders and co-editors of the poetry magazine *Cyphers*, and is a member of Aosdána. Her latest book of poems is *The Boys of Bluehill* (The Gallery Press, 2015).

D Nurkse is the author of ten collections of poetry, most recently *A Night in Brooklyn* (Alfred A Knopf, 2012). His work has received the Literature Award from the American Academy of Arts and Letters and has been shortlisted for the Forward Prize.

Kathleen O'Brien retired early from teaching English to do an MA in Creative Writing, and recently finished her poetry thesis at University College, Cork. She was also inspired by apprenticeships at the Oxford University Summer School for Poetry, and the Seamus Heaney Summer School at Queen's University in Belfast. She is presently working on her first poetry collection.

John O'Donnell is a poet and short story writer. His latest poetry collection is *On Water* (Dedalus Press, 2014). In 2012 he won a Hennessy Literary Award for his short fiction.

Killian O'Donnell's work has appeared in various publications. He lives in Cashel, Co Galway.

Simon Ó Faoláin was born in Dublin and raised in the West Kerry Gaeltacht. He has published four books of poetry. Amongst the awards his writing has won are the Glen Dimplex Prize, The Strong Prize, the Walter Macken Prize, the Colm Cille Prize and the Foras na Gaeilge Prize. He is Director of An Fhéile Bheag Filíochta, an annual bilingual poetry and arts festival in Baile an Fheirtéaraigh.
Rugadh **Simon Ó Faoláin** i mBaile Átha Cliath agus tógadh é in Iarthar Duibhneach. Tá ceithre leabhar filíochta foilsithe aige. I measc na ngradam atá buaite aige dá scríbhneoireacht tá Duais Glen Dimplex, Duais Strong, Duais Bhaitéar Uí Mhaicín, Duais Cholm Cille agus Duais Foras na Gaeilge. Tá sé ina stiúrthóir ar An Fhéile Bheag Filíochta, féile dhátheangach ealaíne bhliantúil ar an mBuailtín.

Caitríona O'Reilly is a poet and critic. She was educated at Trinity College, Dublin where she completed a PhD on American poetry. She has published three collections of poetry with Bloodaxe Books, *The Nowhere Birds* (2001), *The Sea Cabinet* (2006) and most recently *Geis* (2015), which is jointly published by Bloodaxe and Wake Forest University Press. She lives in Lincoln.

Stav Poleg's poems have appeared in UK journals including *The Rialto, Magma* and *Poetry Wales*. Her poetry is featured in *Be the First to Like This: New Scottish Poetry* (Vagabond Voices). Her graphic-novel piece *Dear Penelope* (with artist Laura Gressani) was acquired by the Scottish National Gallery of Modern Art.

Ian Pople's *Saving Spaces* is published by Arc Publications (2011). His first collection. *The Glass Enclosure* (Arc Publications, 1996), won a Poetry Book Society Recommendation and was also short-listed for the Forward Prize for Best First Collection.

Aidan Rooney lives in Hingham, Massachusetts and teaches at Thayer Academy. *Day Release* (2000) and *Tightrope* (2007) are published by The Gallery Press.

David Sergeant lectures at Plymouth University. His poems have been published in numerous magazines, and his first collection, *Talk Like Galileo*, came out in 2010. A collaboration with the composer Martin Suckling was performed last year at the Royal Opera House.

Cherry Smyth is a poet, writer and art critic. She has published three poetry collections, *When the Lights Go Up, One Wanted Thing* (both Lagan Press) and *Test, Orange* (Pindrop Press). Her novel *Hold Still* was published by Holland Park Press in 2013. See **www.cherrysmyth.com**.

Damian Smyth was born in Downpatrick, Northern Ireland. A first collection, *Downpatrick Races* (Lagan Press), appeared in 2000. *The Down Recorder* (2004), *Market Street* (2010) and *Lamentations* (2010) followed, also from Lagan Press. *Mesopotamia* appeared from Templar Poetry in 2014.

Liane Strauss is the author of *Leaving Eden, Frankie, Alfredo,* and *All the Ways You Still Remind Me of the Moon* (Paekakariki Press, 2015). Her poem 'It' won second prize in the Cardiff International Poetry Competition and 'My Last Coyote' was shortlisted for the Strokestown International Poetry Prize. She was the Head of Poetry in Creative Writing at Birkbeck College, and now teaches for Writers House at Rutgers University.

Anne Tannam's poems have been published in literary journals including *The Moth, Skylight47, Boyne Berries, The Poetry Bus* and *Crannóg*. Her first collection *Take This Life*, was published by WordsOnThe Street in 2011, and her second is forthcoming with Salmon Poetry in 2017. Anne is co-founder of the Dublin Writers' Forum.

Tomas Unger lives and works in New York. His poetry has appeared in *The Threepenny Review, Literary Imagination*, and elsewhere.

GC Waldrep's most recent books are a long poem, *Testament* (BOA Editions, 2015), and a chapbook, *Susquehanna* (Omnidawn, 2013). Waldrep lives in Lewisburg, PA, where he teaches at Bucknell University, edits the journal West Branch, and serves as Editor-at-Large for *The Kenyon Review*.

David Wheatley's recent books include *Flowering Skullcap* (Wurm Press, 2012) and *Contemporary British Poetry* (Palgrave Macmillan, 2014).

Nerys Williams's first volume *Sound Archive* (Seren, 2011) was shortlisted for the Felix Dennis prize and won the Rupert and Eithne Strong first volume prize in 2012. Born in Carmarthenshire, and a Welsh speaker, her first volume *Sound Archive* (Seren, 2011) was shortlisted for the Felix Dennis prize and won the Rupert and Eithne Strong first collection prize in 2012. She lectures in American Literature at University College, Dublin.

Macdara Woods is writing and publishing for more than fifty years. His most recent books include his *Collected Poems* (Dedalus Press, 2012), and an eighteen-page pamphlet, *From Sandymount to the Hill of Howth* (2014). A founding-editor of *Cyphers* and a member of Aosdána, he has just completed a new collection.